Sentinels Along the Way
Stories of Inspiration

Sentinels Along the Way
Stories of Inspiration

Compiled by

Doris S. Platt

Distributed by:
Granite Publishing and Distribution, LLC
868 North 1430 West
Orem, Utah 84057
(801) 229-9023 • Toll Free (800) 574-5779
Fax (801) 229-1924

Page Layout & Design by Myrna Varga, The Office Connection, Inc.
Cover Art & Design by Tammie Ingram

ISBN: 1-932280-63-4
Library of Congress Control Number: 2004113230
First Printing, October 2004

Printed in the United States of America

10 9 8 7 6 5 4 3 2 1

To My Father

The word sentinel has many meanings. It may be a watchman, a guide, or a protector. Sentinels can also be key people or experiences which help define our path and guide our course.

For me, my father was such a sentinel. He taught me that fundamental values like integrity and honesty matter, although in my youth I was frequently frustrated by his unspoken insistence that I do things the right way regardless of how long it might take. He acknowledged that shortcuts might save time initially, but I was cautioned never to walk that tempting path, because "You'll regret it sooner or later."

My father understood the worth of the individual. "Who can know what occupies another person's heart; try to be tolerant and perceptive," he would say. Or often suggest, "Is there a more open-minded way to take care of the situation?"

He had an expansive vision of what life was about and I am the thankful recipient of this legacy; the gift has proven to be of great worth. From my father I learned that we are all the beneficiaries of another person's example. We reap where we did not sow, and we plant for others to gather.

This book then is such a 'planting' and gratefully acknowledges the many sentinels in our lives.

She was his mother and I was sixteen. She was powerful, protective, a guardian at the gates over all those who entered her realm. Her strength intimidated me and exemplified all that I could become. She was beautiful, not because she was slender or wore expensive designer clothes, although she sometimes did, but because she knew how to love and to guide with love. I loved her, because she believed in me, loved me and protected me, sometimes from the world and sometimes from myself and from what I might have made of myself had I been left to walk the paths of life without her guidance.

Her home was quiet; that was the best part for me. No one yelled to get what he or she wanted or to intimidate. Oh sure, we all yelled up the stairs or down the street, because that was before home intercom systems were so widely used and it was too hot to walk the distance in the middle of July, but when something was expected or required, there was only the kind of look or that persuasive convincing that occurs between an adult and growing teens.

I was a junior in high school and in love with her youngest son. I was skinny and had short brown hair. I was the kind of pretty that was appreciated mostly by adults and not as often by my peers until later in my twenties. I had nearly failed the 9th grade, was enrolled in remediation courses and had no idea what I wanted to do after high school.

My parents had been divorced since I was a child; my mother, brother, sister and I lived in an economically segregated com-

1

munity. My mother provided for the three of us the best she could, but there were not many extras. As a result of the turbulent youth and teenage years, I had little or no self-esteem. I had potential, but nowhere to go.

My fondest memory of my mentor is as she stood by me in the kitchen while I typed letters on an antiquated machine into minuscule spaces on application forms. I don't remember the names of the schools or even their locations. What I do remember is that she believed in my ability to be accepted to and attend college.

I felt embarrassed by my 1,000 point score on the SAT and the subsequent pre-Algebra and pre-Writing courses I was required to take prior to attending school, but still I was accepted and finished what

without this sentinel in life I would not have had the courage to begin.

In 1993, I graduated with a bachelor's degree in English and Ethnic Studies. By the spring of '95 I had completed a master's degree in teaching from Johns Hopkins University and had accepted my first "real job" as an instructor with the local community college.

Years later I returned to that colonial-style home on Aster Blvd. I remember standing at the door, waiting to be led indoors, knowing that on the other side of the paned entranceway she was waiting for me.

I sat again at the table, where I had spent so many hours, and shared with her all that I had learned and how I had grown. When I was done, she leaned toward me lifting the woven cloth that covered the table where I had placed the typewriter so many years before. Etched into the antique mahogany were the markings of my labored youth.

After a decade of teaching, I still recall the academic and other inadequacies I felt in my teen's. Because of these poignant memories I am able to recognize similar valueless feelings in the behaviors of some of my students.

In the years when I have the opportunity to teach 16–18 year olds, I invariably include a unit about the filling out of college applications and the writing of college essays. Maybe none of my students need me to encourage their introduction to higher learning, but for me, it's the least I can do to help them overcome the sometimes undirected-potential I myself once experienced.

Perhaps now it is I who have become the sentinel, protector of all those who enter my realm, standing at the open gate of opportunity, just as she stood for me.

3

Beachcombing

Pamela Patchet
Freelance Writer

In the 1980s, on a beach in Clearwater Florida, I met a young woman named Kathe. Although we spent only a handful of days together, my life would be forever changed.

I was feeling tired, cranky and guilty. Heavily pregnant with my third child, I was vastly relieved to have a few days away from the demands of my two toddlers at home, but I was also ashamed of my relief. I waddled to the nearest beach umbrella and saw the only person I recognized from the hotel lobby. I shifted my weight from one foot to the other, and debated about introducing myself.

This young woman appeared to be my polar opposite. Typical Type A executive, I thought. Lean and fit, too. She had probably worked out in the hotel gym while I was loading up at the breakfast buffet. I had seen her type before—hard-nosed, driven to succeed. I was astonished to see she had actually brought a briefcase to the beach. Hunched over and writing reports in between bites of an apple, she seemed oblivious to the miles of white sand and ocean stretched out before us.

I hiked my trashy novel and bag of snacks up under my arm and decided to say hello.

She looked up, obviously still deep in thought, then gave me a welcoming smile and introduced herself. My young husband and her fiancé were attending the same course back at the hotel. Kathe invited me to join her under the umbrella, we made some small talk, and then she went back to work, and I to my novel. I took the occasional break and paddled about in the water, but Kathe continued to plow through her paperwork. Eventually I wore her down, and convinced her to join me in a walk along the beach. I carped about how hard it was to look after two toddlers and be pregnant again, how I had given up a good job to stay home. I was here to enjoy these few days on the beach because I'd earned them, I grumped.

I gave Kathe a gentle poke in the ribs.

"Why are you working so hard?" I teased. "What could possibly be so important that you can't leave it for a few days and enjoy the sun and sand?"

Her answer was one I could never have expected.

"I'm trying to finish my degree in psychology before I go blind. I don't really know how much time I have, so I'm rushing to get it finished."

I couldn't think of what to say. Kathe waved off my embarrassment.

"I'm diabetic; that's why I exercise and eat right. And despite everything, I woke up one morning blind in one eye. I had surgery, and six weeks complete bed rest with my eyes bandaged, but my eyesight couldn't be restored. Doctors told me I might lose my sight in the other eye at any time," she shrugged.

I imagined going to bed every night knowing I could wake up blind.

"Oh, it's OK. I've accepted it," she continued. "Actually I consider myself quite lucky, as I'd already chosen a profession that could accommodate me being blind. In fact, it may even make me a better counselor because sometimes other senses are heightened to compensate, so I'd be a better listener. That's why I feel a sense of urgency to finish. I don't want to study this

5

in Braille, though I will if I have to," she said with a broad smile.

Over the course of the next three days, we talked. Kathe reminded me how lucky I was to be having children. She could not risk pregnancy.

"Not only is Larry my soul-mate," Kathe said, "he has three beautiful daughters from his previous marriage. Their mother is an alcoholic and things are difficult for all of them. I just want to give these girls a soft place to fall. I already love them as though they were my own."

As we walked along the sand, she went on to tell me she came from a large, close-knit family and her youngest sister, who was in her late teens, had Down Syndrome and was dying of heart disease.

"No one in our family ever considered her a burden. I cherish every day with her. She is loving and sweet and gentle. I feel blessed to have her in my life."

Katie put her hands on my belly.

"Be grateful for everything you've been given. Tell your children every day how much you love them. Hug your husband. Love the life God has given you. Enjoy every minute of it. I'm so lucky to have found love. I am lucky I chose a profession where I can help others. I am blessed, and so are you," she smiled.

After three days together, my husband and I returned to Montreal, Kathe and Larry to the US. I was still astounded that someone with so many challenges could be so completely and genuinely happy. I decided from that moment on, whenever I felt the urge to complain, I would think of Kathe.

We promised to stay in touch, and did so for a while, but after my third child was born we lost contact. Over the years I often thought about her. I wondered if she and Larry got married, if she lost her sight, if she became a counselor . . .

When I was asked to contribute a story for this book, the first person who came to mind was Kathe. More than fifteen years had passed, but I decided to find her.

I searched the Internet but couldn't find any information on her. Larry still had the same office address, but when I looked up his name on the Internet, Kathe's name wasn't there. Larry had another wife. I couldn't believe she and Larry never married. They seemed besotted with each other.

I wrestled with my conscience, not wishing to intrude, then finally grabbed the phone and called his office, hoping an established employee might surreptitiously answer my questions. To my surprise, Larry came on the line.

"I remember you! You sat with Kathe on the beach under that big umbrella. You two never stopped talking for three days!"

Larry told me he and Kathe did marry soon after that trip to Florida. She retained her eyesight, and became head of counseling at a leading university. She wrote several books, including one for children on growing up with alcoholic parents. Several students who had been suicidal sent her letters of thanks for saving their lives. Larry said she had changed him from a Type A guy to a laid-back, fun-loving husband and father.

"Kathe had the most fun of anyone I ever met who didn't drink." He chuckled, and then added quietly, "We were so in love."

Larry stopped and I waited for him to continue.

"Soon after we married, Kathe contracted a virus that attacked her heart. She grew progressively weaker until the only option was a heart transplant. Luckily doctors found a match, and Kathe had the surgery in the fall of 1991. True to form, she bounced back to her old self, biking 200 miles every week. I could hardly keep up with her! She gave speeches about the importance of organ donations on behalf of all those still on waiting lists . . ." his voice trailed away.

I held my breath.

"She developed complications . . . Kathe passed away on February 23rd, 1992."

I was silent.

"I spread her ashes on her beach . . . our beach, where we rode our bikes together," he said quietly. "I still visit our spot four or five times a year and talk to her."

"She was my Pied Piper."

Larry went on to say that two years after Katie's death, he married a wonderful woman who had known Katie and understood what a remarkable woman she was. I thanked him, and apologized if I had trespassed on his memories. Larry assured me I had not, and promised to call next time he and his wife visited Montreal so that we could all have dinner together.

When I hung up, I again heard Kathe's parting words on that Florida Beach.

"Be grateful for everything you've been given. Tell your children every day how much you love them. Hug your husband. Love the life of God has given you. Enjoy every minute of it. I am so lucky . . . I am blessed."

A Mule Named Vern

Evan Pope
Rancher

It is interesting how different sentinels interject themselves into our lives without ever knowing it.

My adult children had taken a contract to pack into the wilderness area at Table Top Mountain and bid three miles of barbed wire fence. We would have to traverse a five-mile trail to an elevation of 9500 feet. Our task was to transport 150 large wood posts, 1000 steel posts and over 50 rolls of barbed wire weighing 90 pounds each.

And that is how we met a mule named Vern. Vern was born in the Great Cache Valley in northern Utah. He enjoyed more than his share of grass and hay. He spent his time in lush pastures with low fences and understanding neighbors. One could honestly say without exaggeration, that Vern was over-indulged. With no discipline, he grew to the grand weight of 1800 pounds. In his opinion he was king of the valley. His owner mentioned that Vern did not know his own potential.

"Just blindfold him," he said. "He moans and groans and looks for sympathy. I don't have any time or desire to help you; but you can take my mule. He'll work harder as a borrowed mule. Mules, you know, can't stand prosperity."

I came to realize that we pay for most free things. So it was that I approached Vern with a bucket of grain. After eyeing me with an oversized ego that seemed to ask, "What's in it for me?" I offered, "A free twenty-one day and night stay in Nevada."

As we attempted to teach one another,

9

there ensued awkward moments. For instance, Vern did not know his own name. He couldn't understand "whoa" or "git up," but he had one talent I needed. He was big enough to carry large loads a long distance and there are no trains going to the top of the Table Top Wilderness area within fifty miles of Tonopah, Nevada, which is one hundred miles from nowhere.

The moment arrived when Vern was put to the test. When we placed seventy pounds of pipe on his pack he would groan. At one hundred forty he'd let out a mournful "Oooh!" and at two hundred eighty he'd practically lay down. But, when we'd prod and poke him a little, he'd measure up to the task and get going.

Now Vern wasn't the only mule we had to pack. There was the "Renegade." The owner from whom I acquired Renegade had also put in a bid on this fencing job and when he didn't get it he sold us his mule. A lot like Vern temperamentally, but smaller physically, Renegade would also make his way to the top. Unlike the others, Renegade needed 'blinders' on the outside of each eye and a bit more prodding until he reached the summit.

Then there were Gus and Molly. We were fortunate to meet a well-known horse auctioneer who sold us the critters with the proviso, "You can't return them." These two lovable creatures were little; but they could be loaded to their limit without any complaints. After being supervised two or three trips up the mountain, Gus and Molly could be loaded first; they would then leave together and head up the mountain on their own. The guide would have to hurry to keep them in sight. It was pleasant working with Gus and Molly.

From these fine pack animals, I made some interesting observations. Many people we meet along our journey in life are just like those mules. There are the renegades that need a great deal of maintenance. They require a lot of motivation and subsequently equal rewards. Then there are the Vern's. These are they who are highly capable but who moan and groan and lay down on the job. However, with a little prodding, they will eventually get the job done. And then there are the Gus and Mollies. They are the humble and often less fortunate ones. Yet they accept each task placed before them willingly. As they 'reach the switchbacks' along the trail, they'll stop and visit the sick at the hospital; at the next switchback they will do some compassionate service and so on and so on. Quietly they go about doing their jobs in shouldering their responsibility without complaining.

I will probably not return to Table Top Mountain, nor will I work with those animals again. Yet I am grateful for my experiences with Vern, Renegade, Gus and Molly. They qualify as memorable sentinels along my journey.

11

Cameron S. Platt
Police Officer

The best learning experiences often come with a sweet reward or heart-breaking pain. I was fortunate enough to have the "good kind" from my grandfather.

My great-grandfather built a small family cabin next to a river. The location is the closest approximation to heaven on earth for me. The river runs literally feet away from the cabin with a calming, soothing voice. Behind it, a mountain rises up above a grove of pine trees and has provided enjoyment to many generations.

My sisters and I spent two weeks each summer with aunts, uncles, cousins and grandparents. My grandparents were our caretakers. My grandfather was responsible for the upkeep and remodeling of the cabin and was constantly tinkering with one project or another.

The majority of my time was spent fishing. My cousin and I would sit on the bridge over the river for hours on end trying to catch the family breakfast or dinner. The competition was keen and not to be taken lightly.

One day as my cousin and I were fishing, my grandfather passed us on the bridge pushing a wheelbarrow. He asked us to help bring up some firewood from the grove where he had cut down a dead tree. Grudgingly I put away my fishing pole and went to lend a hand.

When I was young, I was a little uncomfortable around my grandfather because he would hardly speak. He had a quiet, gruff manner. As I grew older, I came to understand that he only spoke when necessary and then with the minimal amount of words. Once I learned the rules of his communication, we reached an

12

understanding and I found the silence during work enjoyable.

On this day, we spent several hours bringing up logs and splitting them for later use, such as warming the cabin or roasting "s'mores." When the job was complete, my grandfather said he had something to show me. He took me to look in the back of his van.

Inside was an old motorcycle that he had modified to ride in the mountains. He asked if I wanted to drive up to the reservoir to try it out. I was absolutely thrilled! I have always been drawn to motorcycles and here was my chance! I thought about my cousin still fishing and asked my grandpa if I should go get him.

His reply has stuck with me these many years. He said, "Naw, let him fish." My grandfather was kind to each of us, but on this day, he made me feel special and appreciated.

Joanne W. Mills
Attorney

"If you can't stand the heat get out of the kitchen!" roared one of my law school professors, in response to a classmates' complaint about the burdensome reading assignments we had just received. I don't remember who that instructor was now, but I do know that it wasn't Professor Edmund O. Belsheim.

It was the fall of 1985; I was newlywed and a brand new law student, eager to plunge into the unknown but intriguing world of law. There were many who had tried to dissuade me from going at all, and many who made the going rough once I got there. Then there was Professor Belsheim. Eighty years young, he made the complex subject of wills, trusts and estates come alive for me. He so enjoyed what he was doing, that even the driest legal formulas for determining which surviving heir was the lucky recipient of the testator's sizable fortune, seemed captivating.

Professor Belsheim had immense patience, respect, and love for his students. He never once raised his voice at anyone in class, and kept our study of the dead and their posthumous desires lively with his witty, if old-fashioned humor. I used to love going to visit him in his office to ask about something I didn't understand. I even made up a few questions, if it had been awhile, just to have an excuse to go see him. He made me a better thinker, and always made me believe that I had known it all along, and just needed to be nudged in the right direction. In a cutthroat and competitive profession, he made us feel valuable, confident and full of unlimited potential.

Professor Belsheim hosted a party for

14

students at his home in Lake Oswego, Oregon. We all brought our husbands, wives, friends, and had a blast! I think he was eighty-three by then, but he was so alive, so interested in the goings-on of the world, and, most importantly it seemed, in us.

I will never forget my last day in his classroom. He composed a poem, which he read aloud. It was a witty ode he told to his students, organized into "categories," which he had created. He began by thanking those who had always come prepared, and answered his questions correctly, for we had taught him about excellence and diligence. He then thanked those who had come prepared most of the time, and answered some of his questions, for they had taught him about choices and com-

promise. Next he thanked those who had come prepared only some of the time, and were not able to answer most questions. From them he had learned to be understanding and encouraging. Finally, with half of us in tears, he thanked those who were never prepared and unable to answer any query correctly, for they had taught him patience.

Professor Belsheim remained at Northwestern School of Law of Lewis and Clark College until his 89th year, retired, and joined his late wife not long after. How fortunate I feel that our paths crossed, that his gifts of seeing the positive in everyone, pursuing a lifelong passion with complete devotion, and remembering to laugh about it along the way, were bequeathed to me.

15

David L. Thompson
Interior Design and Decorator

To be asked to recall someone whom you feel made a great difference to your thinking, after six decades, is quite a task, there are so many.

One very good friend who stands out showed me very early in life that you can only reach your goal with hard work and sincerity. He started in a very small way with a market stall, and also played music in all kinds of bands in the evenings. He worked very hard indeed and eventually owned restaurants and hotels and amassed a fortune, but he continued to work long hours.

Even when he became a multimillionaire he put on no airs. He would still speak to everyone in the street, whatever their job or situation. He would lend money to anyone, but he was a businessman, and he would see that he got back the exact sum he lent, no interest charged.

I worked for him, after school, from the age of twelve, sewing potato sacks. We lived in a fishing port on the coast, and he sold masses of potatoes to fish and chip shops. Sometimes at the end of the summer season the payment would still be outstanding. I asked him once how he collected, especially when it involved quite a lot of money. "Send the bill," he told me. "And if they don't pay it after a little while, send it again only double the amount. You'll get your money by return, believe me!"

Another day I asked him, "How do you know when you've made it financially?"

He said "You're there when the bank calls you because they need change!" And this did happen!

16

Working as an apprentice decorator for people of the old school, I was taught a great lesson, 'Take time to do the job well, and remember that you never, ever know it all. You will always learn if you have a mind to." At the end of the day, people should feel respect and pleasure for the amount of work they've given to others, as well as what they have done themselves.

17

Nadine Wimmer
TV Anchor

Often colleagues in a competitive industry conspire, rather than inspire. But I've had the good fortune of working with a woman who's inspired me since I was a high school student.

A high school career counselor suggested I take a field that interested me and call someone I admired in that profession. I don't know why Carole immediately came to mind. But I distinctly remember calling her, explaining I was a student, and asking questions. She invited me to the news station. I headed down in my mom's station wagon for a visit.

That day motivated me all through the college classes, finals and early morning internships. I wanted to be just like Carole.

I eventually got a beginner job at Carole's news station and she took me under her wing. She offered advice and honest critique. Through the years, mentorship has expanded to friendship.

I've come to realize, as much as I admire her professional skills, it's her graciousness that inspires me. Few people will go out of their way to help someone seeking a job similar to their own.

I still want to be like Carole. So I continue learning from her inspiration on and off camera.

GRANDMA EMMA

LouAnn J. Anderson
Quilter

She moved in with us when she was eighty years old, unable to care for things herself. She worried every minute that she would be a burden. And she was— an immense burden to a young family.

She burdened us with the responsibility for behaving ourselves; after all, anything we did would get back to Grandma.

She burdened us with a joy for living, for appreciating little things like sunsets and roses. It was Grandma who built a bird feeder and told us the difference between wrens and chickadees.

She inflicted upon us a sense of belonging—belonging to a long line of important people. Before she came they were stern pictures in seldom-used books. Afterwards, great grandfather Munns was always the man with the blue eyes who raised bees, and the quilts we had snuggled under for years were lovingly stitched by a real great-grandmother with gentle hands that stitched beautifully and also killed chickens!

She burdened us with new words like "scalawag" and made sly hints about current fashion. Grandma was solely responsible for our knees being covered.

A deeply spiritual woman, shortly before her death, she called us all together and talked of her parents, gave us counsel, and admonished us to love each other. We felt the weight of her conviction.

Several days after Grandma's death, a new great-grandchild was born. My small daughter's first comment upon learning of her new cousin was, "Just think! Grandma Emma got to see her very first—before anyone!" Even after her death she burdened us with an understanding of eternity.

May we all grow old with dignity and strength as my Grandma did! And may we, as did Emma Goates Phillips, leave behind a legacy of burdens to bless our families.

19

Valentina Perez
Translator

I'm never going to be like her!" That's what I used to say about my mother when I was younger. "When I'm grown-up I will not yell at my kids. I will not wear just anything to go out in public; I will always wear makeup and look good. I won't be old-fashioned, and I'll be a little more tactful."

At some point or another I think many women have said that. But we can't deny what is inherent. As I get older I sometimes scare myself when I look into the mirror, because it seems that I can see my mother. My voice sounds like hers; I think I dress like her if I'm not consciously making the effort not to do so. We think the same in many, many ways. Of course, if I focus on all the things my mother is and I swore I wouldn't be—then that is scary.

But it turns out that she is an amazing woman. Let me tell you little about her. She had to work as a live-in nanny/maid when she was twelve years old to help support her family. At home she had to share a bed with a younger sister. She grew up in extreme poverty, but managed to go to school and become a teacher. She married the love of her life despite her mother being against it. She had three children all close in age and was always a working mom and the main breadwinner.

When my father passed away after a long illness, she was only forty-five years old and forced to restart her life. She went back to school to become a geriatric nurse. She works, has friends who love her, and is very independent, sometimes too independent. Her children have turned out pretty well, if I may say so.

I don't know how she had the strength

to go through so many years of difficulty. But that is something I truly admire about her. Sure, she's not perfect, who is. I yell at my kids every once in a while, I sometimes wear just about anything to go out in public, I don't always wear makeup and look good, and now and then I find myself being old-fashioned and not too tactful towards other people—but if I can have her strength and determination, especially during hard times, then I can handle the rest.

JAKE

Merry White
Librarian

He was tough. He was stubborn. He was demanding. He had no patience for any sin of hesitancy or uncertainty. And he was the most loving and giving person I ever knew. He was like a Hemingway protagonist, only more richly faceted. I have often wished that my children could have known him better, but they experience him every day—he taught me to be a better person and a better parent. I grew up in one of those families they write plays about. I didn't know that life could be so joyfully embraced until I met Jake and the raucous clan of which he was the patriarch.

He was raised on a farm in Amish country during the Great Depression—too many kids, too many mouths to feed, not enough to go around. Life was harsh and demanding, but in that house there was always laughter and teasing and that certain joy that comes from the wholehearted embrace of all that life is.

He could fix anything, and did. He built a rope tow on a hill on the school campus where he taught and everyone waited eagerly for the first snow. His students loved him; because he knew the best way to teach was to show and to do. Men would return to the school from war, from industry, from success and from failure to tell him how much he meant to them, how much he had influenced them.

All of us in the family adored him and loved to tease him. When my sister-in-law Jeanne and I would put our arms around his shoulders and give him a kiss on the cheek he would gnash his teeth and growl like a pirate.

He was the sort of person who enjoyed setting the stage for the laughter and enjoyment of others, and from that, he derived his own separate joy. We were alike in that we were both a little shy. We held back somewhat and enjoyed watching everyone around us. I think I saw him more clearly because I had some distance, having married into the family. And, I think he knew that I saw him as a whole person, not an icon, and loved him the more for his vulnerability, his disappointment, his humanness. I liked to think that we had a separate bond, I hope we did.

I had learned that Jake and his brothers especially enjoyed teasing the womenfolk around them. On my first visit to the family dairy farm, I walked into the dark barn in sandals. From the far corner I heard Uncle Mike say, "Better slip them shoes off, girlie, they're liable to get dirty in here." Obediently, I started to take them off—to the sound of gales of laughter— realizing quickly that I had been had.

For many summers, we drove to the Maryland shore and spend two glorious weeks camped there, fishing, reading and eating "beach sandwiches"—a dubious combination of whole-wheat bread, and generous application of crunchy peanut butter, (Winnie, my wonderful mother-in-law, distrusted mayonnaise in a camp setting) green peppers, tomatoes, and scallions, all from Jake's garden. They were unbelievably delicious, especially with ice cold beer.

One day, we went "crabbin'." Jake backed the trailer into the water and launched the battered old aluminum boat. Jeanne and I clambered in and we rowed out past the reeds into the quiet waters of the bay. The "skeets" had backed off for the morning and there was an ocean breeze. We lowered our evil-smelling bait into the water on strings and waited for the tug. When the bucket we had brought was filled with our catch, we started back to shore. Jeanne and I were chatting in the stern while Jake rowed. Out of the corner of my eye I saw his old sneaker tip the bucket of crabs. Suddenly the bottom of the boat was alive with a scrabbling mass of pincers. Jeanne and I shrieked, lifting our feet, standing to try to escape, rocking the boat. Jake rocked the boat even more and we both tumbled into the bay, gasping and clinging to the sides of the boat. Jake was doubled over with laughter. "DA- AD!" Jeanne admonished. "Grab those crabs, you girls!" he growled at us, "they got loose."

There is much laughter now around the Jake stories. We all seem to have special memories of ways in which he sculpted our hearts and lives. When I was ambivalent about something and dithering in a way I had back then, he said, "Now listen, Sis. You just decide what you are going to do and then you do it." How often have I used that most discrete definition of integrity with colleagues, friends and children! He also used to admonish me to "Fight back, Sis" when I lamented the inevitable roadblocks that tumble into our way.

The terrible irony is that he fell ill to a disease that would slowly and surely deplete him. He and Winnie traveled west at Christmas time. Part of me knew that he did this to say goodbye. When he came to see me, I put my arms around his shoulders—no Pirates growl now—and we wept.

"I'm so sorry that this is happening to you, Dad. I wish I could take it away . . ."

"I know, Sis." He patted my arm. "There is no fightin' back against this." A few months later, he put his .22 to his temple—not in anger or aggression like some others who take their own lives, but with the same mercy that ends the suffering of a sick or injured animal on the farm. He had had enough. This was no way to live and it sure as hell was no way to die.

Several years later, I traveled with my young son to visit my daughter in college. On one of the beautiful fall days I found myself, like a bird, going from landmark to landmark on the familiar way to the house where I had spent so much of my young adult life. I drove my children to the sunny bluff above the river. When I saw the stone marker, I dropped to my knees and wept like a child for all that I had lost: the husband who walked away, the life we shared and the future I had planned for and counted on, most especially for the man who was more my father than my own sad parents ever could have been. There was his gravelly voice, "Fight back, Sis." Laughing out loud, I embraced my bewildered children, and walked back to the car. My life is what it is. And it is very good. Because of Jake, I always know where to look for joy.

My Homeless Man

Carol Lynn Pearson
Author, Poet

I hung up the telephone furious with my friend Neal. He had resigned from a well-paying job in the corporate world because it was not consistent with the spiritual journey he was committed to. But now, Neal was virtually indigent. He had not been able to pay this month's rent on his modest apartment and his car was about to be towed out of his driveway. And so on the telephone, I had said some pretty harsh things. How dare he go through every penny, believing that faith and meditation will manifest that superior job? How dare he make himself so vulnerable? "I just hope you don't find yourself on the street," I had said. "This is how people find themselves on the street, you know. Homeless and on the street."

That was Sunday. Monday morning I found myself on **BART**, the train that would take me into San Francisco. I was going to spend the day with my friend Sue who was in the hospital for tests. But I was not thinking of Sue as I watched the landscape of the East Bay go by outside the train window. I was still thinking about Neal, and still angry. How dare he get this close to the abyss?

When we reached Embarcadero, the train station I was told to get out at, I stepped off the train. Now which exit to get to the right bus stop? I looked around for someone to ask. No attendant evident. No one nearby at all, except a ragged, bearded black man sitting on a cardboard mat, a white patch over his right eye and a red plastic cup in his hand. I walked in his direction.

"Hello," he said, smiling.

"Hello." I fished out a dollar bill and put it in his plastic cup. I had a habit of giving a dollar to the first homeless person I met in the city and sending a prayer for the rest.

"Why, thank you."

"Can you tell me which exit to take to get to the North Judah bus?"

"Right over there. But where are you headed?"

"Parnassas Street."

"Oh, you're going to the hospital. The North Judah will drop you two blocks away. I say take the Parnassas No. 6. It'll drop you right in front of the hospital. In fact, I'm going there myself right now. Sometimes I watch TV at the hospital for a bit."

He grabbed his cane, folded up his cardboard mat and hid it in a little crevice under the stairs. Before I knew it we had climbed the stairs and were walking together to the bus stop. What in the world was I doing? I was walking with a street person just as if—as if what? As if he was a real human being, as if he was worthy to walk with me, as if he was worthy of doing me a favor. In fact, there he was holding out his hand to me. "I'm Rene," he said.

I shook his hand. "Hi. I'm Carol Lynn. Thanks for your help."

"Glad to."

A neon light began to flash inside my mind. "Wake up! Message from the Universe coming through!"

"How are things going for you, Rene?" I asked.

"Pretty good, pretty good. Lost this eye when I was hit by a truck a year or so ago. Couldn't work. Had to sell my house. One thing led to another and here I am. I was head of a drug rehabilitation program here in the city. Have a master's in clinical psychology from Minnesota. Everybody's just

27

one step away from where I am now, you know. You can lose everything. Nothing belongs to you. It's just things. The Man Upstairs gives you the opportunity to accumulate things, but they're not yours. They come and they go."

My neon light was flashing very brightly. Only yesterday I was yelling at Neal for losing everything, and now . . .

"Yep," Rene continued, "we never know what's going to happen to any of us tomorrow. Now is all we've got. This minute. I just take what comes and keep a smile on my face."

"Rene, tell me something," I said, as we boarded the bus. "You have nothing, but you're much happier than most of the people I'm seeing here."

"Happy? Oh, yeah, I'm happy! All that's important is what happens in your heart."

Rene was sitting to my left. An Asian woman behind me was trying to communicate something to me. "Two quarters. Can you give me two quarters for the bus?"

"Sure," I said, opening my day planner to the thin pouch where I keep my money.

Instantly Rene dumped into his lap the contents of his red plastic cap, a handful of coins and the one-dollar bill I had given him. "Here, I've got it," he said.

"No, no. Here."

Fishing two quarters from his little cache, he reached across me to give them to the woman. "Please. I do this all the time."

Rene never stopped talking. I kept my day planner open and began taking notes as if I had stumbled onto a privileged interview with the Dalai Lama.

". . . It's like we each have a different thing to do in this world, a different point of view, and nobody can judge nobody. The most beautiful piece in all of scripture is First Corinthians, verse thirteen.

'Though I speak with the tongues of men and angels, and have not charity, I am become as sounding brass, or a tinkling cymbal . . .'

I had heard those words dozens of times recited from behind the pulpit, but never as meaningfully as they were recited by my homeless man with shining eyes on the bus that day in San Francisco.

" . . . And though I bestow all my goods to feed the poor, and give my body to be burned, and have not charity, it profiteth me nothing . . . Charity suffereth long and is kind; Charity envieth not; Charity vaunteth not itself, is not puffed up . . . Charity never faileth . . . And now abideth faith, hope, charity, these three; but the greatest of these is charity."

When the bus began to climb the hill, Rene pointed out the window, laughing. "See? I told you we'll know Parnassas when we get there. Like we'll know heaven when we get there. Up! Up! We need to keep looking up. Up is where all good things are!"

At the Parnassas bus stop, Rene and I got off together. As if we were old friends, this ragged, dirty, generous, happy man of the street held out his arms to me, and I embraced him.

"Goodbye, Rene. See you in heaven."

He grinned. "Up, up were all the good things are!"

Neil did lose his car and his apartment, and he is slowly re-establishing himself in the material world. His spiritual journey continuous with increasing clarity and peace. Mine does too, I believe. And, I hope, with charity.

29

From "Consider the Butterfly"
Used by permission of the Author

SOPHIA

Janina Pogorzelski
Journalist

*I*f the lessons of life are learned through the renunciation of fear, a chance meeting in Iceland three years ago taught me to face some of my own. My reluctance to be near water or horses was spurred on by a childhood incident involving a mahogany colored mare with a sharp kick to match her temper. Unfortunately, I was standing by a lake at the time, tumbled into the water and nearly drowned.

If you are visiting an island it is important to know how to swim. In Akureyri, capital of northern Iceland, swimming pools are kept meticulously clean and there are strict rules to follow. My traveling companions insisted that we visit one. While they hurried to take a dip, I was promptly reprimanded by a lifeguard for wearing shoes on part of the concourse and es-

corted back from the plimpsoll line. You have to shower and scrub before you put on your swimming costume to be allowed in the pool, which is much less chlorinated than by British standards. I took a seat by a potted palm and was about to open my book when an elderly lady with beautiful blue eyes smiled and introduced herself as Sophia. She was, in fact, part of our tour group, and this energetic septuagenarian artist with a nimble wit revealed a keen interest in nature, classical literature and swimming. It was as though a field of force surrounded her, a gathering of strength, of willpower.

The next day, after my friends had succumbed to motion sickness in an eight-seater plane on a short "air-sightseeing tour," Sophia was keen to go horse riding.

"Icelandic horses," she stated, "have better suspension then its small planes." Rather than spoil her plans for the afternoon, I accompanied her to a farm near Lake Myvatn, where the stable contained a good-looking charcoal horse and another, tea-colored with a golden mane.

"That one is for you," said Sophia. Briefly I explained why it would be best if she rode alone, but she was having none of it. She had a calm manner that equines respond to and helped me up onto the horse. Icelandic horses are small, sturdy, surefooted creatures, a breed unique to the country. Sophia assured me of their steady gait and encouraged me to put my foot in the stirrup. She was very persuasive. As Sophia and her charcoal mare cantered up the mossy pathway, my first-time on a horse was less swift; it neighed and tossed its golden mane as though there was no hay in the stable. Surprisingly, I remained in the saddle for one very long hour, for the most part with my face buried in the mane. It was perhaps a small fear to conquer in the scheme of things, but it was my own fear nevertheless.

Sophia and I became good friends.

She had been a nurse during the Second World War, tending to both wounded troops and civilians who had suffered at the hands of the Nazis. One day she found herself in the wrong place at the wrong time, was arrested and sent to a concentration camp. Somehow, she managed to survive. After the war she returned to her chosen profession and following her retirement from nursing devoted herself to her art—making exquisitely colorful collages of landscapes as seamless as a painting. She achieved success, exhibiting all over the world. Travel was more than something she

31

adored—she saw it as her life-raft.

"People cannot move on account of their sorrows," she once told me. "I must keep moving forward."

Hearing about her life and the sharpness of her perceptions left a deep impression on me.

She was concerned with some people's willingness to be convinced that the world is a safe place, though she did not embrace bitterness because of what she had endured or that they hadn't the imagination to know what happened to her.

Sadly, Sophia is no longer with us. A woman of sensitivity and discretion who could find ways to assist you so you didn't know you were being helped, she has left a lasting legacy in my life. Meeting her initiated an exploration of my family's exper-

iences during the Second World War, which led to reconciliation with a close relation with whom I had been estranged for many years. She has also inspired me to speak out against prejudice where I find it, not to dignify another's ignorance by remaining silent and to ask myself, how much can we ignore?

In one of her last letters to me, Sophia noted that knowledge is useless without a purpose; she cited Cicero who said that men who know nothing of what has gone before them are like children. As we get older the questions are harder to ask than they are to answer, that is the difference between the old and the young—youth wants to know everything, age wants to unlearn what it knows. Sometimes I take shelter in her words.

Doris S. Platt
Compiler

A person who has profoundly influenced me lives halfway across the world in the Republic of Georgia. Situated in the Caucasus Mountains at the junction of Europe and Asia, Georgia shares borders with Russia, Azerbaijan, Armenia and Turkey. Known to the world as the land of Jason and his band of Argonauts, the legendary Golden Fleece and Princess Medea, Georgia is steeped in myth and centuries of tradition. The country has endured invasions and warfare throughout its history, but the short, bitterly fought civil war of the early 1990s was especially painful. Only a few weeks earlier Georgia had been a part of the Soviet Union. Since the breakup of that huge empire, the new nation had not yet been able to catch its breath. Economically and politically, Georgia faced the task of charting its own

course. Now brother was fighting against brother and none of us knew what the next hour would bring. As in most conflicts there was the regrettable loss of life and property. Families with young children and especially the elderly suffered when government officials had to limit the use of resources. There were lengthy stretches of time without water or electricity. I soon learned not to ask, "Is there hot water?" but to be grateful for any water at all.

In food stores, the shelves were nearly empty and the lines of people were long for whatever remained. We whittled our needs to what was available. It was a common occurrence to wait all night and in the morning see the person standing in front of you receive the last loaf of bread or bottle of milk. People went into survival mode: neighbor helped neighbor, shared, made

33

do, and became quite ingenious in the process. During this uncertain time, the sparse but reassuring sounds of daily life took on a whole new meaning and a kind word and a moment of laughter were of immeasurable value. One day, after an all too short spurt of electricity, my Georgian friends joked that when Government officials turned on the lights and saw how many people were still alive, they quickly turned them off again. Ah yes, the human spirit. We were surviving and we were facing the problem together, but a general uneasiness continued. It was especially noticeable at night, when everything was dark and fear claimed the hours.

Things I had taken for granted, like the solitary crowing of a rooster and the rhythmic swoosh, swoosh of a street sweeper's broom offered welcome moments of normalcy, interspersed as they were with the deep rumble of tanks and the angry staccato bursts of automatic weapons. Every morning I waited for the rooster's challenge to another day, and for the sound of the street sweeper's broom. The woman was amazing.

Neither unaware of the situation nor immune to it, she single-mindedly carried out her responsibility. Danger aside, her commitment was all the more admirable as city workers had been unpaid for months. And she was a Kurd, someone from another nation, and not high on Georgia's social list.

Her voice, dress, and actions were always the same. I could hear her, first from a distance and then more clearly as she came closer. She invariably chided anyone not as dedicated as she in keeping their city clean. Yes, there was a war going on, bringing with it an additional constellation of problems, but was that sufficient reason to litter the streets, if only with the odd scrap of paper or the end of a cigarette? Had the Georgians' justifiable pride in their capital city been destroyed along with their buildings? Not if she had anything to do with it! She would be at her post until it became too dangerous to remain.

Changed circumstances had not changed her. Disruption called for adjustment, not for abandonment. Upheaval, whether caused by man or nature, never justified less than honorable behavior.

Eventually the conflict ceased, and life slowly returned to a more normal cycle. When the rooster crowed no more, I had a feeling that he was probably the main course at a long awaited, celebratory dinner. The visible scars of this tragic time in Georgia's history have almost been erased. There are others which will take longer to heal, but even now the crowing of a rooster reminds me of the dedication of an unpaid street sweeper in the midst of war.

Jay Worley
Bush Pilot

*L*ike Australia's remote outback, Africa and Alaska have their equally remote Bush. The Alaska Bush is a vast expanse of snowcapped mountains, boreal forest and tundra meadows, laced together by a network of braided rivers that meander eventually to the sea. This is a wilderness where roads and highways are non-existent, where in early times, people moved about by riverboats during the summer months, and dog sled during winter. The advent of the modern airplane has radically changed all that. Today, Bush residents have everything from mail, food and fuel to newspapers, pencils and paper clips, flown routinely by bush air services. One individual even had enough bricks airmailed to construct a small home.

My story begins in Nenana, about thirty years ago, while employed by a small commercial air service, plying my trade at the controls of an airplane. This was a time when the Alaska Homestead Act was still in vogue. Under this provision a person could acquire as sizable chunk of Alaskan wilderness, provided he live on the land and improved it by clearing it of trees and tilling its fields for the planting of crops. Like a magnet, the Homestead Act drew a mixed bag of humanity. Families, most transplanted from the lower 48, moved north to what is known as the last frontier, seeking a more "back to nature lifestyle," away from the hustle and bustle of American city life. A few heard the Lord's calling and retreated to the Bush in search of God, while others, some self-exiled misfits, appeared, fleeing from who knows where, from some unpardonable vice. This diverse mix was sown like oats into the Bush, to coexist in one of the world's harshest climates.

Among this eclectic group lived Al, a hard-bitten, cigar chewing, thick as a tree trunk, kind of a guy. Unshaven and foul smelling as he was foul tempered, Al lived a reclusive existence seventy-five air miles southwest of Nenana along the Cosna River. The setting was idyllic—crystal clear rivers, bordered by tall spruce trees, with a backdrop of Denali, the highest mountain in North America.

To me, Al's homestead was like a scar on the Mona Lisa, a blight on an otherwise pristine palette. Al had constructed a crude cabin along side an even cruder airstrip that would make the most skilled, daredevil pilot reassess the modest sum of his paycheck. Up to this point, I thought I could get along with just about anyone; but from day one, the tragic blend of my carefree, environmentalist, tree-hugging personality became cross-threaded with Al's slash and burn, arrogant ego. What followed was the most antagonistic relationship I've ever known. Glaring dirty looks, coarse words regarding each other's faults, and an acrimonious, mucho male attitude, were the order of the day.

To Al, I was a necessary evil that cost him a lot of money. The only good thing I could say about Al was that at one time, he had a mother, but often I had my doubts. Not wanting to get involved in a caustic, cruel battle with Al, I steered as far away as possible from his vicinity, turning down many flights to his patch of ground.

I realized that it was only a matter of time before I would have to bite the bullet and fly into Al's place. That time came one morning in early spring, when I had a call to fly to Fairbanks, pick up a young man and transport him to Al's. As luck would have it, I was the only pilot available to take

37

the trip. The young man in question turned out to be Al's seventeen-year-old son, Dennis. Decked out in boots, Bush pants and plaid shirt, Dennis met me at Fairbanks airport toting a large canvas pack, several boxes of groceries and a rifle. He greeted me saying," Boy, I thought the last school bell would never ring yesterday."

He was a polite, helpful young lad, well groomed and looking forward to a summer full of adventure. I liked him immediately. The thought of Dennis being cooped up with Al for an entire summer, seemed to me a sort of purgatory, but Dennis's enthusiasm for what lay ahead filled my airplane with a sort of mystique fog. I could only hope that Dennis wouldn't be disappointed. I wanted to say, "Hey, Dennis, if you need a fast trip home, just call," but I never did.

The weeks wore on, and in the blink of an eye, the long hours of sunlight began to ebb noticeably. Fall colors started to dominate the landscape. Soon, hunting season would begin, followed by the first day of school. I had managed to successfully steer away from Al's place for the entire summer. I wondered if Dennis had made it back to Fairbanks by some other means. The answer came by phone, requesting a charter to retrieve the teenager and fly him to Fairbanks. Once again, I was the only pilot available to fly the trip; this time though, my curiosity had the better of me. I began to look at this flight as a rescue mission, as well as a chance to find out just how bad or good the summer had gone for Dennis. Upon landing, I was surprised to see father and son standing side by side, arms around each other like two old soldiers. Dennis's pack and rifle, plus a large plastic bag, filled with the summer's accumulation of garbage, stood ready to be loaded aboard.

Al cast a sidelong glance towards me, while in a loud voice he said to Dennis, "Tell the pilot I'll be in to pay for the charter towards the end of next week."

I smiled back a sarcastic, "Don't worry, we know where to find ya."

The engine roared to life. In a cloud of dust and a series of bone-jarring bounces, we were in the air, marginally clearing the trees at the end of the strip. I circled for a last look at the homestead at Dennis's request, before heading to Fairbanks. It was then that I noticed Al standing alone waving up at us in a last farewell. He waved until we disappeared out of sight. I had never seen him do this before—an image that would haunt me for years to come.

The trip to Fairbanks was filled with Dennis's tales of his summer adventures, as I listened in disbelief to stories of him and his dad working together, rebuilding the cabin. Al's first true sharing of memories from his own rough boyhood, in an abusive family.

With the gentle help of his father, Dennis became a crack shot with a rifle, learned to tie all sorts of knots, splice rope, run a trap line, and fish the waters of the Cosna for pike and chum salmon.

Nearing Fairbanks, Dennis told me that he and his best friend were going moose hunting during the coming weekend, the first days of hunting season—one last adventure before school started. If he got a Moose, he was going to have me fly a quarter of the animal out to his dad. I looked at Dennis, with his chestnut brown face. He was no longer the young lad I had flown months earlier, but a young man who, like most, wanted his dad to be proud of him.

39

A few days went by. It was Sunday morning. The news droned over the radio in the background, barely penetrating my subconscious—news bulletin— 'a teenage boy was accidentally shot to death yesterday while hunting Moose with a friend. The names are being withheld pending notification of next of kin.'

I thought of Dennis. It could be anyone. Teenagers' moose hunt in Alaska all the time, lots of them. Yet somehow, instinctively, I knew it was Dennis. It came as no surprise when the phone rang, and a man in a halting voice, asked if I could fly to the Cosna, pick up Al, and bring him to Fairbanks. "There's been a tragedy in the family."

"Was it Dennis?" I asked.

"Yes," came the reply, "but don't tell Al. It will kill him."

I felt sick inside. I flew as in a trance, feeling numb. I remember little of the trip, the usual bumpy ride I suppose. Before I knew it, I was on the ground, walking towards Al, who was seated on the steps of his porch, cigar in hand, coffee mug in the other. Surprised, his face full of questions, he asked, "What brings you here?"

"They want you to come home, there's been an accident."

Al stood up, trying to keep this balance. "It's Dennis?"

"Yes." I knew he knew. It was like some bad dream that you'll never wake up from. Mouth open, tears filling his eyes, Al stumbled towards me, spilling his coffee and dropping the cup. In the next moment we were standing, holding each other, while all the rough edges and all the animosity of the past fell away, like autumn leaves from a birch tree. For an instant the world stopped. I had found the fundamental core of this man, the vulnerable inside, housed in a hard exterior. Dazed, Al walked back to retrieve a few things to take to town. I picked up his cup and placed it on the porch.

The flight back seemed to take longer, yet no time at all. Between tears and long pauses, Al's account of the past summer was a mirror image of the story Dennis had told. We landed. Al, slowly extracting himself from the airplane, said "Thanks," and gripped my hand. We held in a tight embrace for the last time. It was then I told him what Dennis had said; that he had had the best summer of his entire life. Al nodded, "It was the best ever for me too." In an instant, Al was gone.

Until his death a few years ago, Al would request me to fly him, to and fro, the cabin on the Cosna. That short dangerous airstrip was smoothed out and lengthened to over 5000 feet—an accomplishment that Al was proud of, and I, very thankful for. On these flights, the subject of Dennis never came up. There was no need. We both felt Dennis's presence in the silence of our conversations, in the long pauses, while the patchwork landscape slid by, beneath our wings. We were joined together as friends because of young Dennis, who disliked no one.

My experience often reminds me of an old American Indians saying, "Never pass judgment upon a man until you've walked a mile in his moccasins." For me, this saying carries more weight than gold.

41

Kaitlyn's Corner

Sonia R. Peltzer, M.D.

*H*er sweet-sad smile made me stop and hold my breath, waiting to glimpse some higher wisdom she seemed to innately understand. Her eyes touched my soul.

Kaitlyn was my first angel. A wondrous, loving angel who caressed the shriveled souls of doctors and nurses and students like me, thirsting for meaning, trying to make sense of the suffering we fought. She was only two months old.

Kaitlyn was admitted to the hospital for evaluation on my first day of pediatrics call as a medical student. When I held her, she seemed so small, so fragile. Fleeing to the library, I searched for a diagnosis that would explain her high calcium and poor weight gain. The innocent plea in Kaitlyn's eyes made the responsibility of finding answers for her weigh heavily on my heart.

But it was the holding that changed me; I simply had to have her in my arms. While her parents stole short snatches of sleep, the nurses would watch over Kaitlyn and I was always there, ready to cradle her in my arms. Her smile seemed to say, "I won't be here long. Love me now, before I go."

Kaitlyn rarely cried; she was serene, peaceful, with blue eyes reflecting the strength of the soul within. When we performed invasive tests, tears would gather for a moment, but then her smile would return, forgiving us.

Within a week, her diagnosis was confirmed: a rare genetic disorder that would eventually cause her brain to swell as her skull fused together prematurely; a disorder that she would not survive. I witnessed her parent's heartbreak, their tight hold on the elusive hope for a cure, and I slowly adopted her family into my heart.

When Kaitlyn died at six months of age, the entire pediatric nursing staff attended her funeral, helping to fill the church overrun with family and friends. Tears flowed like rivers, their turbulent waters building in the united strength of our outpouring.

The church emptied of mourners as the processional to the graveyard began and I waited in my car, sweating in the bright hot Virginia sunlight, assaulted by the heat of summer. It seemed out of place, at odds with the dark chill of my mood—for how can one make sense of a child's death? How can one find warmth after this kind of loss?

Watching Kaitlyn's parents climb into the limo that would drive them to their daughter's grave, I made a vow. Someday, my office waiting room would have a com-forting corner stacked with toys and pillows and books, and overhung with a plaque that read "Kaitlyn's Corner."

Time passed. I entered residency. I had children of my own. And yet I always remembered Kaitlyn; her smile haunted me. When my practice began planning for a new building, my dreams for Kaitlyn's Corner, a space where children could play, watched over by an angel, became focused.

But shortly before the practice broke ground, I gave birth to my third child and my plans were put on hold. Sammy was sick and there were times I thought we might lose him, times the future seemed a fog of uncertainty. It was during those times that I remembered Kaitlyn and her parents. They had held her and told her of their love for her—no matter how many tubes and wires were attached to her little body—insisting that she know the warmth of their touch in the chill of the hospital.

43

They showed grace in the face of a terrible, heart-wrenching reality; comforting me, comforting the nurses and the doctors who could not see how important her precious, short life had been. They recognized the gift of Kaitlyn's life and though they grieved terribly, they survived their daughter's death.

Over time our family was given several incorrect diagnoses and finally, the emptiness of no diagnosis. The frustration of not having an answer was a terrible blow. I listened to colleagues who exhorted me to be Sammy's mother, not his doctor, and my impatience with the medical community grew as he worsened. Sammy was floppy; he nursed poorly and remained under the 5th percentile for height and weight, and as his development lagged further and further behind, I pressed the doctors for an explanation.

"He's one in a million," I was told. My husband and I were doing all that could be done for him, they said. The neurologist and geneticist reassured me that Sammy did not have a genetic disorder. My need to know was urgent. I was pregnant again and we decided to proceed with the pregnancy, believing our little girl would be healthy.

Sarah was our gift, the fulfillment of the doctor's promise that I'd have a healthy child. But a month later, Sarah began to have difficulty nursing, more severe than Sammy, and she aspirated breast milk into her lungs. We returned to the Pulmonologist.

"It's one of those things; we'll never know. She's just like Sammy."

Things don't "just happen." My mothering instinct sped me home and kept me awake as I researched aspiration in textbooks and explored the Internet. Shortly before midnight, I made the diagnosis.

Sammy and Sarah had Familial Dysautonomia.

Familial Dysautonomia is an Ashkenazi Jewish genetic disorder as common as Tay-Sach's disease, with a carrier rate of 1 in 27. It's devastating, progressive, and fatal. Ten years of medical training and practice, and I had never heard of it.

The shock of the diagnoses nearly tore our family apart. What held as together was the belief that Sammy and Sarah came to us for a reason. I am blessed daily by their presence in my life. Sammy's unique compassion, the tender and open matter in which he looks at the world reflects wisdom beyond his years. Sarah's spark of life, the innocent way she embraces each moment are the delicate petals that perfume my world. All of them give me—give all the people they touch—a glimpse of the divine. They teach my heart the truths that Kaitlyn whispered to me years ago.

Kaitlyn's time was measured in months, but her impact on me will last a lifetime. Through Kaitlyn, I learned the importance of holding and loving a child, of gathering the precious moments to your bosom because you never know how many you'll have. She has made all the difference to me as I struggle to mother Sammy and Sarah the best I can.

Kaitlyn's parents knew that it's not the length of life that matters—it's the depth of love that it can hold—and Kaitlyn's well was bottomless. My own children offer the world the deep springs of love that run through them and I'm comforted in the knowledge that whatever the future holds for them, the world is richer for their presence.

There is no office waiting room with a plaque for Kaitlyn, but Kaitlyn's corner exists where it has always been, in my heart.

45

June O. Anderson
Registered Nurse

Late in 1982 as I was driving to Presbyterian Hospital in Denver, Colorado, where I worked as a Registered Nurse, I prayed, as was my practice, that I would be made aware of those whose life I was to touch that night. Little did I realize that I also would be greatly blessed by the experience that was about to unfold.

I was assigned to care for six patients that night, one of which was John (Jack) L. Swigert, a retired NASA astronaut. He had been on the 1978 Apollo 13 mission, which became known as NASA's most successful failure; where he had literally stared down fear.

On that mission Jack and his fellow astronauts, James A. Lowell, and Fred W. Haise, had found themselves on a literal mission of survival. That day, April 17, 1970, NASA scientists, engineers and the three astronauts entered a race against time to save the crew of the crippled spacecraft. After the parachutes were deployed, as planned, and the space cone, ˜Odyssey, splashed down in the mid-Pacific, the astronauts were picked up by helicopter and transported to their recovery ship, the USS Iwo Jima. A prayer of thanks was offered and a passage from Genesis in the Bible regarding the creation of the world was read. The words were spoken, "God bless all of you—all of you on this good Earth."

Jack had accomplished much in life, and was loved, revered and respected by many. However, his concern that night was with an indescribable pain throughout his body, which had brought him to the hospital earlier that day.

Upon entering his private room, I felt an immediate bond between the two of us.

Our kinship continued to develop that night and the next. He had been given several medical tests and expressed concern what they might show when they became available the following day. I asked him, as I often did when prompted, if he was a prayerful man. He warmly responded that he was. When I asked him if he were Christian, he also answered affirmatively and requested that I join him in prayer on his behalf.

We shared a few sacred moments, then I knelt at the side of his bed and, at his request, offered the prayer. I asked Heavenly Father to be with this great and humbled man as he faced the future. Jack had a remarkable quick, creative mind, but in this he would have to rely on faith.

As I arose from that prayer, tears streamed down both our faces. We both expressed gratitude for our belief in God. After our prayer, he slept comfortably through the entire night. He was still asleep when I completed my shift.

Returning to the hospital the next day, I learned that I had the same patient assignments as on the previous night. When I entered Jack's room, our eyes locked with deep and mutual understanding. We both knew that he had been diagnosed with advanced bone cancer. He requested that I offer another prayer asking Heavenly Father for the strength to withstand what was ahead of him with grace and dignity. He also requested that we thank the Lord for the life and accomplishments He had given him. We again shed tears of gratitude and once more he slept through the night.

Jack was released from the hospital before I went to work again. He had won a

47

seat in the U.S. House of Representatives from Colorado's Sixth Congressional District with 64% of the vote. On December 27th, 1982, one week before he would have taken his seat in Congress, Jack L. Swigert died in Washington D.C., due to complications from cancer. His body was flown back to Colorado where I attended his funeral.

I was blessed to have met, cared for, and learned from this truly "Giant of a Man."

As a boy growing up in Winnipeg, Canada, when it was still a frontier town where one stepped off the boardwalk straight onto the prairie, to belong in that vast, wild land rather than the London where I was born, was terribly important to me. My proudest accomplishment was to be a Boy Scout, and a good one. I learned all the skills I could master, and was pretty pleased with my ability to read maps, survive in the wilderness, find drinkable water, track animals, make a fire, put up a tent and tie all the knots known to man. I felt I had really earned advancement.

When the scout master I most admired refused it I was crushed. I felt humiliated and angry; it was hard to face him, or my friends. Naturally I protested.

"Oh, you're good at all those things," he said to me. "You're strong and fast, you're bright, and you learn quickly. You've got any amount of courage—but Bowman, you are unreliable!"

Unreliable! I crept away in silence to think about it. He meant I could not be trusted! When I was needed I might be there—but I might not. If you were in trouble and called for me maybe I would come, maybe I would give all I had to help, be wise and brave and kind—but maybe I wouldn't.

It was a terrible thing to say. If that were true, then what use was I?

Alone in the starlight on that vast prairie that seemed to stretch to the end of the world, I swore an oath to myself that never again, never in all my life, would anyone be able to say that of me. Come heaven or hell, and everything that lies between, I would stand fast to my word. No one

49

would ever think they could rely on me and when it came to the crunch, find me not there.

I have made mistakes, some of them I regret deeply, and I have certainly not always been right, but I have never forgotten that scout master's words or the mark they left on me. Through my years in the army in World War II, and afterwards, I strove to keep my promise to myself. Stand fast! May those who rely upon me find me there and ready always.

Marie-Louise Strehlau McMullen
Retired Aide to Congressman Wayne Owens and Congresswoman Karen Shepherd

As I look back to the winter of my eighth year, I can almost feel once again the penetrating cold and dampness which seemed to be everywhere.

My mother had just died, and to make matters worse, we moved to another city in Ohio, a city on Lake Erie where the winter winds coming off the lake brought unimaginable cold.

The move meant that I was uprooted from everything that was a part of a child's security, familiar room, neighbors, school, and most of all, my friends.

Going mid-term into a strange classroom with an unfamiliar teacher, and being the "new girl," was like a nightmare.

Even on that first day, I was aware of one little girl who was different from all the rest. Instead of the curious stares from all the others, this child met my eyes with a friendly look and a warm little smile.

After class she came immediately up to me and introduced herself in the most adult way, and from then on we were friends.

How she could have understood my misery, and then reacted to it, is still a mystery to me all these many years later.

Mary was poised and mature beyond her years, and became the model which I was to emulate as soon as my family became acquainted with her. I heard over and over, "Why can't you be like Mary?" Or, "Mary wouldn't say (or do) that."

Instead of my resenting the comparisons, I loved her dearly, and tried my best to be like her. Because of her warmth and unselfishness my grief was easier to bear. She took me to her house where we played for hours with paper dolls, each of us having a shoebox full of the dolls and

51

clothes we had cut out from a Sears catalog.

I had never attended Sunday school on a regular basis and she took me to her church every Sunday, establishing there and then a habit which has not ended. I even wonder if my interest in antique dolls and miniatures was not born when I stood in front of her wonderful dollhouse, or when I played with her magical Bye-lo doll. (I now have a dollhouse of my own, and four Bye-los.)

Speaking of Bye-lo baby dolls, Mary had been given one for Christmas and wanted show it to me, so she got her mother to bring her to our house the day after Christmas. I was smitten with this wonderful doll, and Mary handed it to me so that I could take it upstairs to show my big sister (who was now the mother of the family, because she was twenty-two years

old.) I tripped running up the stairs and accidentally smashed that dolls head on one of the steps. I began to cry, but Mary comforted me instead of her crying. I can still hear her words as she patted me, "That's right. That's all right."

My sister was furious with me after they had gone, and dragged me downtown to the department store to buy a replacement head. I got lectured AND lectured, all the way there, and all the way home. But I shall never forget eight year old Mary comforting me.

Thanks to Mary, I gradually changed from a shy and lonely child to one that eventually became more like her. That little person set me on a path of gentility which I might not have known until much later.

When we moved from the city by the lake after only two or three years of there,

Mary and I kept in touch through letters for many years. We grew up and married, she married a doctor and I married a minister. We had babies about the same time.

Not too many years ago she came to visit me, and I told her about how she had influenced my life. She was surprised, and completely unaware that any of her actions had changed me.

Would I have become the person who cares deeply for others had I not been given an example years ago? It's hard to say! I'm happy that I was given the opportunity to tell her, and to thank her for having been my friend at a time when I desperately needed it, for not long after that visit my Christmas card was returned as "addressee unknown."

Thank you, Mary Mendenhall Morton, wherever you are.

Uncle Vin and Aunt Marge

John J. Huebner
President, Mor-Lite, Inc.

My Uncle Vin and Aunt Marge meant a lot to me when I was a little boy. Some of my fondest childhood memories are from times spent with them. Whenever I went over to their house I knew I was in a safe place where nobody would yell at me. They always made me feel welcome and treated me like one of their own children.

Aunt Marge always seemed to be making something good to eat and I could have all I wanted. I have a vivid recollection of her warm and comfortable kitchen; the way the counters were laid out; the window at the sink where she stood; the dog's food and water bowls; the swirly pattern on the linoleum floor; the way Aunt Marge looked with her apron on. She was beautiful.

She always made me feel good about being there and that somehow everything was going to be OK . . . and that I would be free from harm.

She knew about a faraway place called Belgium. There was always something interesting going on . . . a project to do, something to build, even a game to play . . . jigsaw puzzles, too. It was a fun and fascinating place. They had a dog named Bozo that would chase his tail and do tricks Uncle Vin taught him.

There is a lot of talk today about male-role models and how important they are to boys growing up and not having an easy time of it. Uncle Vin was mine. He taught me a lot. He taught me how to hammer a nail by holding the nail close to the head, not at the bottom . . . so I wouldn't smash my thumb. Boy, does that hurt. He taught me the secrets of how to paint things so that the paint job didn't end up looking like a big mess.

He taught me to punch holes in the bottom of the lip of a paint can so that the excess paint would run back inside the can instead of down the outside and all over the place. Even now, some forty years later, I think of my Uncle Vin every time I open a can of paint, and it's like he's there with me, making sure I get it right.

He taught me the miracle of removing a flywheel from the gasoline engine of my motor scooter by placing a two-by-four against the end of the shaft and whacking it with a hammer . . . magically popping it loose.

He taught me to think, to work toward solutions to hard problems that I didn't understand, and not to give up until the answer was found, but if the answer wouldn't come, to not be afraid to ask somebody.

He taught me to take my time and do it right the first time. Just about all of the hands-on mechanical skills I possess started with my Uncle Vin. When he said "Take and do like so," I knew it was time to pay attention. He would patiently show me the right way to do something. He taught me to not quit until the job was done . . . no matter what.

He was a big man, known for his strengths, with big capable hands that guided me. I can see his hands to this day. He could fix or build just about anything. He taught me to be honest and always do what was right . . . that's what policemen did . . . they were on the side of the right.

When he came over to our house it was a major event . . . a time for excitement. Sometimes he would chase my sister and me, laughing uncontrollably, around and around the house until I was laughing so hard I couldn't stand up. Sometimes I even wet my pants I was laughing so hard. My sister probably did too, but she didn't say.

He would back his police patrol car up the driveway so that he could get away in an instant to save the day for someone in need.

He was my hero. My Uncle the policeman. None of the other kids had one. He wore a real gun and he even let me touch it once. I was disappointed that he had never shot a bad guy.

He would run the cord from his police car radio to the inside of the house, so that he could stay in touch with what was going on. I got to listen to all the very official-sounding police conversations coming over the radio.

Just after high school I moved far away to go to school and make a life for myself. I've always felt badly about drifting away and losing touch with my Uncle Vin and Aunt Marge. I've always felt their presence though, and I will carry forever the influence they had on me as a kid who needed all the guidance he could get.

The lessons I learned from my Uncle Vin about not quitting until a job was done; about how to find solutions to tough problems; and about finding honor and satisfaction from working with my hands, have all stayed with me. They are a permanent part of my life and a major source of enjoyment.

Seventeen years ago, some friends and I started a lighting company using a new, energy efficient technology. My friends were all bright business executives with prestigious college educations. They knew a lot about how to put together complex financial and investment deals. They knew how to work with computers when very few people did. And they knew how to manage big and complicated operations.

The problem was that none of us knew much about lighting, or how to make the light fixtures actually work. After a few years, the company was going nowhere and they handed it over to me asking nothing in return.

Every day, for two years, using many of the skills my Uncle Vin taught me, I wore a tool belt full of tools, and spend a lot of time on ladders and scaffolding in grocery stores, office buildings, and textile mills, trying to find solutions. Twice, I lost every penny I had.

It took years of struggle, but my uncle had taught me how to keep working and not give up until the job was done. Today, my company's lighting equipment operates in over 250 manufacturing plants all across the United States and in Canada, Mexico, and several South American countries.

The patents I applied for have been granted and my company is prospering. I've met and married an incredible woman and now live in Park City, Utah in a home overlooking a lovely meadow with the mountains beyond. We've just completed a three-month major remodel and construction of our new home.

I did a lot of the work myself using the skills Uncle Vin taught me and I thought of him every day. Uncle Vin died last month . . . a peaceful death, mercifully. Every day is an ache and an emptiness, but at least I have the wonderful memories of some of the best times of my boyhood spent with him. It's been that way for over fifty years now. Of course it's not the paint or the can or the nail that matters, but the time he took and the love he showed me when I needed it most.

I owe a lot to my Uncle Vin and to my dear Aunt Marge, too.

57

Garabed A. Tahmazian
Petroleum Geologist

*I*t did not take very long for me to identify the person who had a great influence on my life. I met Hikmat George Shlah in Calgary, Alberta, Canada, in the spring of 1965, shortly after I finished my graduate work in the U.S.A. and started my career as a petroleum geologist. He was an immigrant from Iraq who came to Calgary to study and became a master electrician. We quickly formed a strong friendship. Not only could we speak Arabic together but we had many interests in common.

By the summer of the same year he was ready to marry his sweetheart, Debbie, a lovely and charming Lebanese immigrant, whom he met in Calgary. I was delighted when he asked me to be his best man.

Both of us began to raise our respective families. Hikmat proved to be a terrific friend, husband and father and was highly respected as a master electrician. He was hard-working and disciplined and lived his life with a set of values rooted in his Christian tradition. Hikmat was a gentle giant. I say that because he was a 240 pound muscular man who became the youngest champion wrestler in his native country of Iraq. Yet he was soft-spoken, had a keen artistic eye and a great sense of humor. He enjoyed music and traveling, he had a great curiosity for ancient ruins and history along with an endless zest for life. My wife Doreen and I traveled often with Hikmat and Debbie and had marvelous times together.

In the late eighties he was diagnosed with kidney cancer, and one of his kidneys was removed. A few months later he was operated on to remove a cancerous rib.

Shortly after that, he was diagnosed with inoperable lung cancer.

His only chance was to undergo two weeks of a dangerous and very painful course of experimental chemotherapy in the intensive care unit of a Calgary hospital. Upon completion of the first course he was asked if he was prepared, after two weeks rest, to go through it again to improve his chances. True to his tough, tenacious personality he agreed and this time it proved to be more difficult, dangerous and extremely painful. Then tests showed that the cancer was miraculously gone. Although they were no guarantees that this difficult cancer would not return, Hikmat continued to live life to the fullest. He was checked regularly; but ten years later signs of the cancer showed up in his lungs once more. Again Hikmat, with the support of his wife, family, friends and his doctors, who continued to call him their miracle patient, rose to the occasion saying, "I am going to beat this thing."

He went through several painful operations, including an exploratory and two more lung operations and one to remove a cancerous lump on his back which was painfully close to his spine. The cancer spread to his brain and he underwent a series of radiation treatments. Finally, with an inoperable lung cancer, and another tumor on his back and having to take a handful of experimental drugs by mouth every day, his magnificent muscular body was reduced to a skeleton. Yet the day before he died peacefully in the hospital, he was determined, even though it was a monumental struggle for him, to travel to another facility for an interview with a specialist about a bone marrow transplant, telling the doctor "I am going to beat this."

In December 2000 my friend Hikmat died. Throughout his thirteen years of ordeal he beat the odds, kept his spirit up, including those of his loving friends and family who were so worried about him.

During his remission, Hikmat visited many patients who were suffering from the same disease, to encourage them and lift their spirits. I feel so privileged, honored and fortunate to have had him as friend. His courage in the face of adversity and overwhelming odds and his faith in God will remain a special guide to me as to how to live, love and die.

I have been extremely lucky to find myself in the company of good friends, and at times strangers. The acts of friendship and kindness that I have encountered no matter how small the gesture I can honestly say have been from those who truly loved and cared for me. Throughout my life I strive to do the same for others. I have my grandmother Ida to thank towards helping me become the person I am today. She is no longer alive but is very much alive in all that I see and do. I owe my life to her as she sacrificed a great deal for me.

I was born in Italy in a beautiful charming village called San Biase high up in the foothills of the Matese Mountains in a region known as Molise. My mother left me when I was six months old along with my sisters, to be cared for by my grandmother and aunt, while she left to join my father to work in a textile factory in England in order to support us.

One morning I had difficulty breathing and was seriously ill. The nearest hospital was over an hour away down the mountain and across the valley to the nearest town. Only one bus left the village each day and my grandmother had to run for her life clutching me in her arms to the piazza to commandeer the bus, which luckily had been running late that morning. She pleaded with the bus driver and passengers to take her to the hospital as quickly as possible. Her resolve and sheer determination and diplomacy ensured she made it there in time for the doctors to operate and it was her action that saved my life.

She later brought my sisters, aunt and me to England when she helped raise us until I was nine years old and then returned to Italy. I had the opportunity to

61

visit my grandmother in the village on many more occasions before she died. I recall spending my eighteenth birthday helping her tend the vines in her vineyard that was also home to a huge fig tree. She asked me what I wanted for my birthday and I said I had all I wanted as I was there with her but that a fig would be nice, and before I knew it she was up the tree picking as many figs as she could. We sat under the shade of that tree and ate fresh figs. I had the best birthday one could wish for.

My grandmother had a big heart and she shared with us her home and great sense of humor. Ida in all her wisdom had a great respect for life and nature and lived frugally from the land she loved, farmed and cultivated and taught me all she knew. She not only loved me but she had firmly planted and given her children, grandchildren and great-grandchildren their roots. Just like one of her vines or olive trees she tended and nurtured me, protected my fragile roots, and carefully prepared the soil to provide me with strong foundations. Ida never asked for anything in return, and continued, for as long as she was able to tender and nourish us, her dear little plants in all seasons and weather. Her faith never floundered and she never judged us. Ida enabled me to grow and survive and become healthy and strong in spirit. Ida helped us to bear such fruits as love, compassion, integrity and respect. These are the things she taught me and that have shaped my character, and I am lucky to surround myself with friends who share and mirror these qualities.

Daniel Stashower
Author, Magician

*I*n 1973 I fell under the thrall of a television program called "The Magician," which chronicled the adventures of a headlining performer named Anthony Blake who solved crimes on the side. Blake lived on an airplane, drove a white Corvette and had some emeritus status at Hollywood's Magic Castle. Each week we learned there is no situation so perilous that it cannot be mastered by the skills of a really good magician.

On one location, Blake witnessed an attempted mob hit while scuba diving—the blond victim was tossed into the water in heavy shackles. As fate would have it, Blake happened to have a set of lock-picks in his diving suit—in his diving suit, mind you. Another episode found him tracking down an evil drug lord, who showed his displeasure by leaving an angry rattlesnake on the passenger seat of Blake's Corvette. With his magic-heightened reflexes, he managed to stun the snake into submission with a flashy silk production.

I was thirteen years old at the time, and struggling to master such basic magic tricks as the Linking Rings and Multiplying Billiard Balls. Anthony Blake's crime-solving, airplane-dwelling lifestyle looked pretty good to me. I read everything I could about magic and magicians. I spent every weekend downtown at Snyder's Magic Shop on Public Square. I practiced my card fans and coin rolls for hours at a time in front of a full-length mirror.

One morning in late October my grandfather called with news of a magic show at Severance Center, the local shopping mall. Did I want to go? It seemed unlikely to me that a real magician—a crime

63

solving, snake-thwarting magician—would ever be found at Severance, the chief attraction of which was a Slurpee machine. Still, I insisted on arriving an hour early, so as not to miss anything. I kept watch at the fountain, near the Hot Shoppes, while my grandfather drifted off to buy razor blades. The fountain was shut off and a riser platform had been thrown up to form a makeshift stage. There was a gold-edged lobby card sitting on a wooden easel. It read: "Quantrell the Magician."

After a time, a man I took to be Quantrell arrived and began setting up his equipment. He wore an ivory-colored leisure suit with glitter at the lapels, and a pale green tuxedo shirt with deep ruffles. He had the first Zig-Zag cabinet I'd ever seen. Also some brass rice bowls, a wooden duck bucket and a silver Zombie ball. I'd been told, at Snyder's, that the Zombie is what separates the great ones from the rest of the pack. That's the one where a big silver ball floats up off a pedestal and peeks over the edge of a silk foulard. If you can do that one—at close quarters, with an audience on three sides—you had the goods.

When he finished setting up, Quantrell walked over and said, "You must be a magician, am I right?"

I admitted that I had been known to do a trick or two, now and then. "I was thinking of starting off with doves," he said. "I do a bare-hand vanish. What do you think?"

I said that sounded like a pretty good idea. Quantrell nodded. "But I also have some Hippity-Hop Rabbits ready to go," he continued. "I could always start off with that. What do you think?" No, I said, the doves sounded just right. He nodded again, as if impressed by my wisdom. "All right," he said, handing me his business card. "Thanks."

The show started about half an hour later, and Quantrell's bare hand-dove vanish was exquisite, I thought. He moved smoothly through some rope and silk tricks, then launched into the Zombie. As the silver ball floated up and perched on the edge of the foulard, Quantrell looked out over the crowd and gave me a big wink. I believe I waved back. I may even have saluted.

I still keep Quantrell's business card in a red-lacquered Mystic Ball Vase on my desk, along with several others I've been handed over the years—Ricky Jay, David Copperfield, and the late, great Harry Blackstone. People sometimes ask me who in my opinion is the best among the magicians working today. I couldn't really say, but I do know what separates the great ones from the rest of the pack. For me, Quantrell the Magician, late of Severance Center, is the one who had the goods.

65

I Am a Military Brat

Cindy Davis Castleberry
Estate Manager

My father was a career military man. He was only 16 years of age when he volunteered for the Korean War. Thankfully, someone soon found out his age and brought him straight home from the front lines in Korea (just in time, I understand his entire battalion got wiped out one week after his departure). Later, yes, of course, he was sent to Vietnam once; then he volunteered to go back a second time. Why? Well, just because he couldn't leave "His Men" over there, he had to get them out. He was to me, not once, but twice, my hero. He brought home Bronze and Silver medals all in a bunch; which quickly became play toys for my cousin, but to my father they represented a job well done and more importantly he was home. We joked with one another about how much of a "gunhoe" Joe we had in our family: everything we owned was Army green; our car, our house, our bedrooms and living room! You could say our favorite color was "Green"! However, when we spoke of patriotism, our love of family, country and yes, God, we were certainly not "Yellow"! Please, pardon the expression, but in our home one could say it was the best of times and it was the worst of times (1960s).

Because of my father's career path, we were required to move to a different military base each year to eighteen months. This lifestyle proved to be challenging for one as young as I. However, each time we moved, we were given the opportunity to "go back home to Georgia" even if just for short period of time. Well, my Mother is one of thirteen children and my Father is one of four children, so you can only imagine how big our family reunions are! When we all got together it would be the men in one room watching ballgames and the women in the kitchen cooking up something good and the cousins trying to stay out of mischief! It was during these times that discovered who I was. This is where my strength, my direction, and my sentinels shine through. I discovered my history; learned that my hair was as dark as the grandmother's I had never met, that I was the most like my aunt Ginny, the rock of our extended family. I learned where I could go in life and that I had people who loved me, believed in me, and no matter what, gave me unconditional love.

Yesterday and today, the sentinels in my life are my family and my extended family. There are too many to name, yet so many to love. I thank each one of them for making my life a better place. I do love each one of them.

SENATOR MARGARET CHASE SMITH

Deedee Corradini
Former Mayor of Salt Lake City, UT 1992–2000

*I*t was 1959. I was 15 years old. Our family had returned from 11 years in the Middle East—Lebanon and Syria—had spent a sabbatical year in Massachusetts, and had settled in Brunswick, Maine.

As a junior in high school, I had experienced difficulty in adjusting to life back in the United States. Having grown up in the Arab world, having traveled extensively throughout the Middle East and Europe, and having been accustomed to seeing and discussing world problems and issues, it was hard to fit into an American teen culture focused on American Bandstand.

Rather than spend time with high school classmates, I was more interested in spending time accessing the benefits of nearby Bowdoin College and all that it had to offer—lectures, plays, and competitive

swimming occupied my time outside of the school day.

Having grown up in the Middle East, I knew that I wanted to make a difference with my life, and thought that some form of government service might be in my future. Our United States Senator at the time happened to be the only woman in the Senate. I admired Senator Margaret Chase Smith— not only was my given name Margaret, but she carried herself with such dignity and intelligence. The rose she always wore on her lapel added to her beauty as a person.

I wrote her a letter one day, telling her of my admiration, and a little of my background and interest in government and international affairs. Much to my surprise, she wrote back. Her message was personal, and her point was that I should pursue my interests and that I could do whatever I aspired to.

That small gesture on her part inspired me for years to come. After earning a Master's degree, I went on to work for a Governor, worked in the U.S. House of Representatives, got elected twice to serve 8 years as the Mayor of Salt Lake City, and became the sixth woman in over 60 years to be elected President of the U.S. Conference of Mayors.

My only regret is that I never had the opportunity to meet Senator Margaret Chase Smith. When she died, I felt a twinge of personal loss.

One person can make a difference!

69

Jamie Stone
M.P. Scottish Parliament, UK

You stroll along a life of local politics —not too big issues, and bigger lunches—and then someone does something that shows you something higher. With me it was real courage. And it was my late father's old friend Harry Miller who showed me.

This lady, from a 'traveling family', lived in appalling conditions in a remote cottage in the Highlands. Her children had an incurable hereditary disease that would ultimately kill. Her husband was in jail for violent crime.

The local council—chairman of housing, one Harry Miller—decided to buy and adapt a new home for her, one that was nearer neighbors and medical support. This happened—and then the cold shadow of a local vigilante group blotted out the sun of help and care.

"We don't want these types of people living here!" Petitions were signed, poisoned letters were written, abusive telephone calls were made—and one by one the elected members of the council's housing committee were picked off. Just before Christmas the game was up; as the snow fell the majority was no longer there— and the lady was never to get that house. Even today, she is still in the same lonely spot.

But Harry Miller never wavered.

"We are all God's children" he said. He lost; support that he had counted on buckled to the left and the right of him—but he carried on. In the end he voted—very publicly—for that family to have that house.

I know the private abuse—indeed evil itself—that he endured. And he never flinched. It was lonely; it was courage of the highest kind; and it was inspirational.

Harry has been dead for five years now. But, though he failed, he deserves to be remembered.

One of the most fascinating aspects I have found as I listen to my father reminisce is that his stories provide vignettes on life and people he met through the years, which apart from memory would otherwise be lost. One such example describes a beautiful afternoon in a quaint little village in rural Northern Ireland in the mid twentieth century. The Mid Antrim Hunt of which he was a member had decided to meet at noon in the village of Ahoghill in County Antrim. Picture the scene if you will, blue skies, warm sunshine and a gentle breeze, with about twenty or so mounted individuals each fully attired in the appropriate dress for both the era and the activity that lay ahead. Here in this small square among the group gathered was Lady O'Neill, wife of the future prime minister of Northern Ireland, Lord O'Neill, himself a descendant of the High Kings of Ireland. She was riding sidesaddle as only a lady would and immaculately turned out in the English style as always. Surveying the events from behind their lace curtains were the formidable McDowell sisters, standing in the drawing room of their home.

As a boy my father had visited there with his mother, and remembers being delighted when they opened the wall safe to present him with a silver biscuit barrel full of delicious treats! However, this particular afternoon a surprise was approaching, Lady Moyola, wife of another future prime minister of Northern Ireland, rode into the diamond. She had decided to ride that day wearing full Western Cowboy gear from Stetson to spurs, much to the astonishment and chagrin of some of those present. One

71

can only imagine the raised eyebrows of the McDowell sisters as they watched the new arrival jaunt into the village!

My father had a rather wonderful and formidable cousin by the name of Jesse Bannatyne Wilson. She was born in the year 1856 in the city of Limerick on the beautiful and rugged West Coast of Ireland. Her father, the Rev. Dr. David Wilson, was a much respected moderator of the General Assembly of the Presbyterian Church and served in Limerick for fifty years. She married in 1890 William Ryves Poe and went to live at Cloughmoyle Castle, Shinrone, King's County, now County Offaly set in the rolling hills of Southern Ireland. Unfortunately her husband, from an historic family, died childless within a short time of the marriage, and so Jesse lived on as the window in the castle for over half a century.

A great lady, she remained somewhat Victorian in her style and attitudes even into the middle of the 20th century. When Jesse sent her cards at Christmas time, instead of writing on them which was considered impolite, she placed her visiting card inside. She would always carry a rolled-up parasol through out the year, a lighter color in the summer and darker in the winter. She would give sweets to the children of the village in her walled garden much to their great delight. Family members recall their visits when young, in particular playing with marbles on the uneven floors of the castle. Their favorite room was the one in which the marbles would roll back and forth across the floor, eventually coming to rest in the center.

Modernity sailed past Jesse or perhaps

she glided right through it. She continued to travel by horse and carriage, never owning a car, and used oil lamps and log fires long after electricity became popular. For all the years of her widowhood she had two companions, Dick the coachman and Maggie the housekeeper. These two individuals lived together 'below stairs' as if they were husband and wife. After about twenty five years, one day sitting together at the kitchen table Maggie said to Dick, "Well, what about marriage?" There was a considerable pause, allowing Dick enough time to reflect upon his life—past, present and future, and finally he thoughtfully replied "Maggie dear, there is no one good enough for either of us." And so life in the castle continued just as before, for another twenty five years!

It was those stories and also his recollections of our forebears that inspired me to develop my great interest in and love of people. My father, now approaching 90 years of age, both loves much and is much loved. He is noble and gallant, with tremendous personal honor and integrity. He is of an immensely practical nature, a gentle man who is very forgiving and abundantly generous. He retains a witty sense of humor, despite the vicissitudes of his life, and as his son, I have never known him to let me down in any way. His word is his bond, and he has shared with me the finest principles. I am blessed much more than these words express to have the individual I have, as my father. He stands as the greatest example of what a sentinel represents and will endure as such throughout my life.

I would like to mention another

individual who I feel ranks as a Sentinel. Some years ago I visited and stayed with his Royal Highness Duke Christian Ludwig of Mecklenburg. He was born in 1912 at Ludwigslust, the Summer Palace of his father, who was the last sovereign Grand Duke of Mecklenburg-Schwerin, one of those now vanished countries that once formed the German Empire. He was connected to all the ruling houses of Europe and he had a unique Slavonic ancestry stretching back some one thousand years to Niklot, Prince of the Obodrites.

Despite his ancient lineage and industrious heritage I found him to be a courteous, gentle and intelligent man. He spent many hours relating the events of his life and reviewing albums of family pictures, both peppered with significant happenings and notable people of the last century. He recounted in detail his trials and tribulations through the Second World War period and the following seven years, which he spent in the notorious Lubyanka KGB prison in Russia. However he never failed to mention such details as the capable British brigadier who protected valuable historical artifacts at the royal palace in Schwerin. This was during a chaotic time when occupation of the palace and the surrounding area changed from British hands to Russian and back to British administration within a week. He also talked about a humane commandant in Moscow.

Duke Christian Ludwig did not criticize nor condemn, merely affirmed how fortunate he was and how others suffered far more. He was without guile, and his modesty and humanity will remain with me as an abiding memory of goodness. It was a privilege and pleasure to know such an individual who exemplified sincerity and steadfastness in all things.

Through experiences of my own and those of others, I firmly believe that one day we shall know just how significantly we touched the lives of others, whether it be a chance meeting as fleeting as the wind or that of a lifelong friendship. We are all capable of empowering others to know of their greatness also. And we all can stand as sentinels enriching our own lives and inspiring our fellow human beings to the good that is within of us.

THE STORY OF GRACIE

Chris A. Redgrave
VP/ General Manager
Radio Broadcasting Company

I grew up in Canada in a hard-working family with a strong sense of character and determination. I loved both parents very much, but I was especially close to my mother, Grace. As a young woman my Mom had decided she wanted to attend the nursing program at Toronto University. This was against her parent's wishes, as they wanted her to get married and have a family, but my Mom was bound and determined to have both.

She was accepted at the college and shortly after graduating she met my father Victor and married him. They had three children-myself, my older sister Joey and younger brother Paul. When I was nine years old we emigrated to the United States due to my father's employment.

The Midwest accent, the flat wide-open spaces of Oklahoma, and leaving family and friends behind must have been hard on my mother, yet she never complained. I distinctly remember thinking we would return to Canada and that Oklahoma was temporary. Who could blame me? This area of the country proved to be a challenge for my family. One day in May of 1968, I was home by myself when a friend of mine ran up to the house and said, "Chris, come quick, it's Paul." We hurried to the rivers edge and found out that my brother Paul was missing after heading downstream on a makeshift raft. The river was swollen with strong currents due to spring runoff, and the last thing my brother had said to one of his friends was that he couldn't swim, but not to tell anyone.

The search went on for hours and my Mom finally returned home completely exhausted. My father stayed by the river in disbelief. The divers found Paul's body that night. I was the first one back at the house. My mother saw me and ran out on the front porch. I wanted so much to bring her better news, but all I could do was shake my head. When she realized what had happened, she collapsed. My father was never the same after the tragedy. In fact at his funeral in 1994 his friend spoke and said a light had gone out in Vic after Paul's death. My Mom was equally devastated, but she found some strength within her for our sakes and went on with her life still honoring my brother yet being present for my sister and me. Her strength and her sense of responsibility were amazing. What

in this world can be worse for a parent then to lose his child.

As a young adult I fell madly in love with Danny, a U.S. Navy Seal. He introduced me to the intoxication of the Hawaiian Islands. We did it all. He was a diver, so we dove for fresh fish and lobster. He loved skydiving, so we jumped out of airplanes. He owned a plane, so we flew around the islands. Three years later when I was working at the Pearl Harbor Naval Officer's Club one of Danny's diving partners came to the club. He said I needed to go with him to the ship they had been working on. When I arrived on the scene I knew Danny was gone. He had been the victim of a number of mishaps surrounding the job. My Mom took the very next flight to be with me. She had adored Danny and it was her strength and resilience that kept me from thinking that my life was over at the age of twenty-five.

My mother continued to teach me with her courage after she was diagnosed with the blood cancer that eventually took her life. She never pressured me to be something I wasn't or made me feel I was a disappointment. Her constant message was "you can be anything you want to be, if you put your mind to it." She would also say "there isn't anything you can't accomplish." This attitude required unconditional love because I was a late bloomer and a female version of Peter Pan. I did not want to grow up. My Mom's demonstration of love for family and friends, her passion for world travel, personal integrity with commitment to her word, a strong sense of humor and her work ethic lives in me every day . . . It's what I strive to be. In June of 1994, I had the ultimate honor of being present at the time of my mom's death. I held her hand as Gracie slipped peacefully away.

Jaclyn Nicole Fleischer
Junior High School Student

It was the first day of kindergarten. I was so happy to be going. I made a lot of friends, but my best and most favorite friend introduced me to a whole new world, the world of horses. Lindsay just loved them. I did not know a lot about them, but she did. One day she took me to the farm where she rode, Brown Wood Barn, the farm that was right next to my house! I love being with horses, they are so much fun! Lindsay got me started in what I love now. I plan to be a horse veterinarian one day. But I would not even have known about any of this without Lindsay. I now have three horses of my own and have been riding for eight years. It's still fun!

79

Ty Nielson
Junior High School Student

When I was three years old our family moved to Moscow, Russia, for my dad's work. We lived in Moscow for two years and then we moved to Vladivostok and lived there for three years. That is where I met him. His name was Dema. I called him "Deemchick" that was a nickname in Russian that meant like my buddy Dema. I met him because he came to our church one day. Members of our congregation had met his dad on the street. His dad was crying because his newborn daughter was very sick in the hospital and they didn't have enough money to buy the medicine to take care of the baby. We gathered up some money and took it to the hospital, but it was too late, the baby died. But Deemchick and his mom and dad came to church. He was a little, dirty blond haired boy with **BIG** blue eyes that would

just pierce you. The instant I met Deemchick, we felt a bond. He didn't speak English and I didn't speak really good Russian, but we loved to be together. Dema was always up for anything, riding bikes, playing video games, climbing trees; he specially liked taking baths at my house. He didn't have a bathtub, bike or video games, so it was fun to share with him. When he would leave my house I would always give him one of my toys because he didn't have very many of them. His apartment was very small. It was one room for him, his Mom and Dad. When I left Russia, I gave my bike to Dema because he had never had a bike. The smile on his face was sooooo big. The night before we left Russia our friends had a party for us to say goodbye. When we left that dirty building and my family was driving back to our apartment I said to my Mom and Dad (I was eight years old by then). I said crying, "It doesn't matter how dirty or yucky someplace is, what matters is that we have our friends." That is what Dema taught me. That where you are just doesn't matter, what matters is the friends you have. I hope that someday I can go back to Vladivostok, Russia, and find Deemchick again.

How My Life was Changed

Harvey Jason
Antiquarian Bookseller

They say that miracles happen to people who believe in miracles. That may indeed be true, although I'm not sure I ever counted myself among those believers, Saturday, June 28, 1997 was the day I got sick and tired of being sick and tired. And because of that I became the recipient of what I call a miracle.

For many years of my adult life I thought the solution to all the pressures that came my way was to be found in a bottle of hundred-proof vodka. It took me a very long time to realize that alcohol, far from being the solution, was in fact the problem. And that's what finally hit me, in a single-and stunning-moment of clarity, on Saturday, June 28, 1997. That morning, slumped in defeat and self-pity at the desk in my study, head pounding relentlessly from alcohol abuse of the night before, mouth parched dry as sand, there, with curtains drawn against the sun's blinding intrusion, I asked G-d for help. Really asked Him. With all my being. Asked Him to relieve me of the compulsive obsession to drink. I'm convinced my prayer was heard. And answered.

I was almost immediately led to a program of recovery. It's been said that there are no coincidences; the coincidences are simply G-d's way of remaining anonymous. I subscribe to that, and in this case I believe that's what happened. Resulting from my introduction to this recovery program my life truly changed. Almost immediately. In every way. I realize that by relieving me of the compulsion to drink, G-d has done for me what I could not do for myself. I am, today, free from this addiction. And I have been given a way of life, and design for living which, if followed, will allow me to continue to live in G-d's grace. To live a tranquil and serene, joy-filled, productive life without the need for any artificial embellishments.

For me the spiritual connection is the most important thing. I have always been an observant Jew. I treasure my Judaism, and I treasure my relationship with G-d, a relationship which has become infinitely more personal. I talk to G-d regularly, and I know that when I talk to G-d, that's called prayer. (I also know if I hear him talk back to me that's called schizophrenia!)

Levity aside, I try to live each day with the absolute, ongoing awareness of His divine benevolence and love. Realizing that each day, every day, what I'm given is a gift. I'm not entitled to this; it's a gift. And a gift, no matter how beautifully wrapped or decorated, doesn't do much good until the package is opened. So every day I have a conscious and very real awareness of the ingredients of that gift. Each morning I relish the twenty-four hour period ahead of me. I no longer, as I did for many years, live in the past, in all those yesterdays, nor do I live in the future, in all the supposed tomorrows. I'm aware that there may not be a tomorrow. I have no guarantees. (If I want a guarantee I'll buy a toaster.)

I'm privileged to live in today. In the Now. I've not only been able to make amends for bad past behavior but I've also been given the awareness that if, for example, I feel guilt or shame or regret over an experience long gone, then I'm living in yesterday; if I feel fear, I'm living in tomorrow. Thank G-d, I can now live happily, freely, and gratefully, in the day that I'm in.

And that simple word, gratitude, is for me the key to it all. My experience has shown me that gratitude is the one emotion which cannot coexist with any form of negativity. If I'm grateful, I can't be resentful, I can't be self-pitying, I can't be envious, I can't be depressed. I can only be happy. And I have been given happiness. For so long I thought that happiness was an objective towards which I could strive. I was wrong. I now know that happiness is not an objective. It's a bi-product. A bi-product of a way of life. And I've been given it.

So today my life is happy, joyous and free. Yes, of course there are bumps in the road, challenges of all sorts, issues of ill health, deaths of those we love, the coming to terms with one's own mortality, yet this is life, and I learned that life can't be lived on my terms; it has to be lived on its own terms, on life's terms.

I am so blessed.

As I prepared with my family to celebrate Independence Day, I realized how fortunate I have been in my life. I doubt that the special people in our lives were put there by accident. My Grandpa Hanson definitely was a special sentinel in my life. He was a simple American boy born George Leonard Hanson on December 12, 1903 in a small town called Kane in upstate Pennsylvania. His parents were Swedish immigrants and he was the oldest of eight children. Tall and handsome he had a twinkle in his eye and an air of authority about him.

Grandma Maples said she was seventeen and he was nearly eighteen years old when they met and fell in love. He was a machinist for Holgate Manufacturing Company there. They were married on Jun. 3rd, 1924 and had three children; two boys and my mother, Margaret Louise.

Grandpa became the foreman of Holgate's and later on the superintendent there until he resigned and bought a Western Auto Store in the town where I was to be born, Greenville, Pennsylvania. Because Holgate manufactured toys along with wooden handles and other things, Grandpa was able to a hold Christmas party every year and would take many of the toys they made to the orphanage on the New York State border. When he owned a Western Auto Store in Greenville, his was the biggest toy store in town. At 5:00 PM every Christmas Eve he would close the store and ask someone at the Salvation Army to come and pick up the all the remaining toys that had not sold to be delivered that evening to the needy children in the area.

Family members recall often seeing hobos and homeless men during the Depression years. They would come to

85

Grandpa's house or business. He would talk to them and if they wanted to work, he would invite them into his home to wash up and eat and he would give them odd jobs. He always lifted people and helped them to feel pride and dignity. My Grandpa taught me so much about compassion and unconditional love. I could see how others were drawn to him, to his warmth and humor, his integrity and wisdom and his strength of character.

Grandpa loved baseball. Years after television was highlighting the games, I would still see Grandpa listening to them on his old radio. He was a fan of any good game, not really rooting for any one team. When I was seven he taught me how to throw a baseball (like a boy) and to swing the bat. Much to my mother's dismay, he also taught me how to "spit." He had a huge maple tree in his front yard in Greenville. He only had to show me once how to climb that tree. After that I became obsessed with tree climbing. The trouble was we had moved to the Pacific Northwest where the trees were taller and full of sticky "pitch." I often was asked to remove my clothing before being allowed into the house after a day of climbing.

Grandpa was a simple All-American man with a heart of kindness. He loved God, his family, his country, hard work, little children and animals. Children were drawn to his warmth and love and I remember being jealous a few times of the attention he gave to all. Because I lived on the West Coast and he lived on the East Coast, I didn't want to share him even with my cousins when we would be reunited. I remember my mother counseling me on sharing him with the other children and to always remember that he loved me. He made each of us feel that he loved us the most.

Grandpa Hanson sent me my first bicycle. It was my sixth Christmas morning of the year 1954. I woke up to a shiny new green and white 24" Schwinn two-wheeler! Wow, I sat on that bike all day and walked it around until I learned how to ride it the next week.

When I met and fell in love with Kevin, my husband of 35 years, Grandpa told me to always try and support my husband with love and faith. "Go where his opportunities might be and be willing to move your family and make new friends." He encouraged me to get into banking when Kevin went to Vietnam and was stationed on an ammunition ship for four years during that war. His advice was always loving and sound and supportive. His politics were conservative. His leadership was profound. And he had a way to find humor in nearly everything in life.

When Kevin was given a job opportunity in Utah it was Grandpa who encouraged me to be happy to move our four little girls away from family and friends in Seattle—"to give it a try and to think of it as a new adventure."

He passed away in November 1983, but he leaves a wonderful legacy to those of us left behind. God bless this great man and all that he contributed not just to my life but to countless others and to his own prosperity.

REFLECTION

Mary Klein Bowers
Account Manager

*M*y Dad was a businessman and an athlete
He was a scholar and a prophetic and thoughtful writer
He was a friend to many, and a lover to one
He carried a silent strength and was a hero to me.

Even today, I find myself calling on his strength,
Seeking his wisdom and asking for his guidance and forgiveness.
Wishing I could have one more day.
Just one more special day

I continue to explore how man lives his life,
How that will define him when he is gone,
My dad was a man who lived a good and honest life.
He was wealthy in friendships and respect and love.

In reflection, one should not be measured by bags of gold,
but rather the lives he touches and holds.
My dad was a great and humble man
I reap the benefits of his life daily

He lived his life without hate,
Pure of malice,
He honored life by creating good,
This is significant and should be held in high esteem.

To grow and be nourished,
To be adored and loved, simply because you are you, is a gift.
A precious gift cherished day to day.
My dad gave this gift to me.

He is gone now but his spirit and love remain.
I am a better person because of him
I try to live my life with care and in his memory
He is still my hero.

Barbara Yaros-Mitchell
Retired IBM Executive

To me, she was the quintessential grandmother—kind, patient, self-sacrificing, hard-working, humble, honest, sincere, sweet-natured—and a visionary. Her name was Margaret Hoefer, and she sailed from Mannheim, Germany to Ellis Island, New York with her sister, Johanna, aboard the Bismarck shortly after the turn of the 20th century. She married William (Willie) Herrschaft in the early 1900s and enjoyed a union that flourished for decades until he drowned in Cold Spring Harbor, New York, in 1958 while fishing with a group of friends. Margaret also survived the emotional wrenching of the murder of her beautiful sister, Johanna, who was shot to death on the streets of New York by a crazed gunman in 1907.

Margaret, or Gretchen, as she was called by her family and closest friends, was a remarkable woman. In the 1920s, she applied for a driver's license and drove her own car when most women did not do such things. She opened a small grocery store in Bronx, New York at a time when women did not own their own businesses. The shop failed because of her overly generous heart—she would not force customers, who were already struggling financially and who owed her money for the groceries, to pay their bills. Consequently, Margaret could not pay hers, and the store closed.

Realizing the importance of being literate in the language of the country she now called home, she taught herself to read and write English. There were no night classes back then; there were no home study courses. It was an overwhelming task, but she succeeded brilliantly, even managing to sound American-born and to write proficiently with great fluidity—yet another remarkable achievement for this diminutive, incredible powerhouse of gentleness and kindness. She was proud to be an American.

Margaret gave birth to four children: Charlie, Bill, Eddie and Madeline. She and Willie proudly nurtured them into adulthood. In 1938, I was born to her daughter, Madeline, just eight weeks after my grandfather's tragedy. This is where my extraordinary experience with my grandmother, known to us children as "Grossie" short for the German word "Grossmutter" (for Grandmother) began. My birth, I was later told, helped ease the great pain of Willie's loss.

Grossie loved all of her grandchildren equally, not favoring one over the other. This exemplified the way she lived her life with all those passed through it. I have never known a more fair, less non-judgmental person then her. As far back as I can remember, she was always there for me with her guidance and support.

When I was three, Grossie showed up at our doorstep with her little overnight black satchel which she had brought from Germany. We had no telephone; she had no telephone (most families didn't,) but she just knew something was very wrong. She felt it. She took the train from the Bronx to Brooklyn where we lived. She was "right on": my parents were in bed severely ill for several days with the grippe (known today as the flu or virus) Grossie nursed them back to help. They healed quickly, and she was on her way back to the Bronx again.

There were many instances of her prescience. She had asked her husband not to go fishing that fateful day. She had a dream the night before the outing that he was

91

swimming in blood. Willie allayed her fears by saying, "Margaret, I'm the best swimmer in the group. Actually I'm the only swimmer. I'll be fine." What neither of them could foresee was the fact that the heavy lambs wool coat he wore on that bitterly cold day could not be easily unbuttoned when the boat capsized. The garment filled quickly with water and dragged him to the depths. He was the only one who drowned that day.

My 16th birthday was the most fun time I ever had. Grossie took me to Florida in celebration of the event. We left on a streamliner from Grand Central Station very early in the morning of an icy February day. We awoke to the warmth of the Georgia sunshine on our way down to the Sunshine state. The sudden contrast in temperature over such a short period was dramatic, and I remember that feeling till

this day. It was the first time, too, I saw Spanish moss hanging from trees in the swamps of Georgia, and, until we arrived at our destination of St. Petersburg, I spent as much time as I could in the open air of the caboose.

It was the happiest time of my life. For nearly two weeks, I was treated with great kindness, thoughtfulness and respect, so different from the topsy-turvy turmoil of the home environment left behind. For the first time I knew what relaxation and freedom from fear was like. We laughed a lot, too. I will remember that time all the days of my life. I slip into those moments intellectually when times get tough.

Grossie also fostered my love for the celestial. To escape New York City's intense heat, summers were with her and the grandkids, nieces, nephews, et all, at Grossie's summer home at Round Top in the Catskills. Every summer she would have the children watch for the Northern Lights (aurora borealis), allowing us to stay up as late as midnight outdoors to watch for this predicted phenomenon. Mosquitoes would bite; the air got cool, but we diligently watched for those northern lights, hoping and praying they would show. I don't recall ever seeing the lights, but it sure was fun waiting and watching.

What I do recall is Grossie quizzing us children periodically on where to find the Big Dipper, the Little Dipper and the North Star (Venus). To this day, I can locate those constellations in the heavens. She once took us to the famous Hayden planctarium in Manhattan where I first saw our galaxy represented by an incredibly-designed model hanging from the ceiling. Once I even thought of becoming an astronomer, but my math wasn't great. For me, following Hubble's happenings is a favorite pastime.

Margaret was a deeply religious woman who loved God and lived her life daily by the Golden Rule. All who knew her loved her. There was never an unkind word spoken about her. How could you criticize a saint?

Her words, repeated many times, will ring within my ears forever, "You are a good child—very, very, good." What a thrill to hear that from the woman you admire and love the most. Grossie gave me the faith, hope and desire to believe in myself. That indeed is the most priceless of gifts.

The memories of Margaret are endless and boundless. She was, is, and forever will be, my Guiding Light—my Sentinel Along The Way.

Martha Williams
Attorney

Writing a story about a person who made a difference to me, someone who acted as a guide post along my journey is a great thing to ponder! I realized that there are so many, some with bigger roles than others. It brought home to me the importance of every day, of being kind to all you meet, because you never know what role you will play in a stranger's life.

When I was a little girl, I had a strong and loving connection with God. I felt His love, and wanted to do His will. I even considered becoming a nun when I grew up, though I also wanted to marry and have children.

When I was 16, my mother developed breast cancer. We children knew she was seriously ill, and the radical mastectomy, followed by radiation treatments, was very hard on her. Through it all, she was a tower of strength for the whole family. What the doctors told only my dad, and which we learned many years later, was that with eleven positive lymph nodes, she had only a year or so to live. My parents were devoted to each other, and this was a hard to burden for my father to bear alone.

Our family moved to San Antonio, Texas, shortly after my mom's surgery. I found it increasingly hard to go to church. It didn't help that the new priest, who I now think was an alcoholic, never had a kind word to say to teenagers, especially the girls. I decided I wanted nothing more to do with such a God, who would allow my wonderful mother to suffer so much, and to have such cruel representatives. I left the church and didn't pray, not even when my mom developed serious heart trouble caused by the radiation treatment.

94

Years went by. I finished school, started working, married and had children. I returned to church with my husband and children, but always with a reservation in my heart, which I think was caused by fear and mistrust. When asked in a personality test if I preferred justice or mercy, I chose justice, however harsh, because at least that would be fair, as opposed to mercy, which I saw as arbitrary and capricious.

By some chance, I started reading the Brother Cadfael mystery novels, set in the England of the 1140's. They were lovely little stories, beautifully written; they made the people of long ago came to life. I read them all. Halfway through, it dawned on me that Brother Cadfael's God wasn't a harsh tyrant, but was like the God of my early childhood. Something in those stories broke the ice around my heart, and I started on my journey back to my loving and merciful God, who had been with me all the time that I'd had my back to Him.

So, although I never met Edith Parge-ter, who wrote the Brother Cadfael novels under the name of Ellis Peters, I will always be grateful to her for her mystery novels, which pointed my way back to God.

As for my mother? She never did have a recurrence of the cancer that threatened her life so long ago. She and my father just celebrated 50 years of marriage.

Foray into East Africa: Surgery, Exploration and Insights Were on the Menu

Bhupendra C. K. Patel

M.D., F.R.C.S., F.R.C. Ophth

"*Polé, polé, sasa,*" a popular African song intones. "Take life easy" is the refrain, and certainly, along the coast of East Africa where we operated in March 1999, life is undertaken at a leisurely pace. "How was Africa?" Many friends and patients inquire.

"Fine, thank you" does it scant justice. The experience demands a more satisfying response.

My son, bwana dogo (small boss, aka Neel), knew he would be making a surgical trip to Africa with me when he turned eight. He also knew he would have to work and he made a decent stab at learning the rudiments of Swahili, the local lingua franca. The trip was a long time in the planning. September 1998 plans had to be shelved after the August 7th bombing of the American Embassy which left 12 Americans and 253 Africans dead, 5,586 injured, many of them seriously. The delay turned out to be propitious as the African bug bit my other two children. The deal was struck at the beginning of the year: if the younger boy (jumping bean Jay) was able to read a 200 page book cover to cover, without pause or potty break, he would win a ticket. As for Tara, then five, well, I have been unable to refuse her much and she won her ticket with a simple smile, albeit a smile that could light up a coalmine.

Travel took us well nigh on two days, via Amsterdam. The two squirts read "Kenya: Africa's Tamed Wilderness" by Burch and "Kenya: City and Village Life."

I re-read Isac Dinesen's "Out of Africa" and "Man-Eaters of Tsavo" by Patterson who probably knew my granddad as they worked together on the Great Railway. The weather en route was fine, the planes on time; the auguries, in short, were most agreeable.

The first day was spent getting acclimatized: Mombasa is four degrees south of the equator. The sun came up each day like a yellow rose and fell like a sweating orange. It was 94 degrees on the first day, 92 the second, 96 third, and so it went. Rivulets of sweat coursed down your back as soon as you stepped out of the shower. The monsoon rains came in the early morning, operatic, exuberant and overwhelming. The mosquitoes, one of God's less likable creatures, sensing a foreign delicacy, sought us out in preference to the local fair and did their daily dozen on our sensitive skins. Mosquito sprays all around.

The clinic we worked in is the same one I've had the pleasure of working in many times. Although no Moran Eye Center, it comes with serious credentials, which it carries with becoming modesty. The corrugated proof, peeling paint and the sparse interior belie the work done there: 140 patients seen every day by one or at most two surgeons and over 2,000 surgical cases a year. When the boys spend time with me in the clinic, we saw a cornucopia of diseases.

Diseases tend to be advanced but demand ceaseless vigilance if one is to avoid being caught off guard. A corneal scratch turned out to be a corneal worm which we delivered alive and well: we housed it in a jar and named it Musa after the clinic administrator. A lacrimal sac swelling was Burkitt's lymphoma, a chalazion was actually a sarcoid granuloma and a young man's sudden loss of vision was caused by potent local brew. Although patients with facial problems where recruited to see us, the spread of word locally attracted all sorts. I saw a patient with burns and even one with anal atresia. The seriousness of some of the pathology was distressing.

My wife came to the clinic as well and summed up the situation perfectly. After we had seen to Juma, the eight-year-old with blindness on one side and severe visual loss on the other caused by glaucoma she uttered "this is terrible" or some such. Five minutes later we saw Samuel, his 7-year-old brother who also had glaucoma with advanced vision loss on both sides and cataracts to boot. "This is most unfair, I thought glaucoma is supposed to affect the elderly," my wife exclaimed. Indeed. This is predominantly so in the Western World. In Africa, glaucoma is six times more common than in America. Astoundingly, 35 percent of patients with glaucoma in Africa are bilaterally blind and 90% are unilaterally blind (as compared to four percent in the U.S.).

They were not simple cases and I wondered what my colleagues Crandall or Durcan might do: I could have profited by their skill and advice. The only image I was able to conjure was one of Crandall mopping the floor between cases, as is his wont. It didn't help and I made mental notes to have words with him on my return. Unenlightened, I operated on Juma's only eye and for the few days we were in town following surgery, he did well. Their father, who looked prematurely aged, didn't move a muscle during my postoperative discussion, but then, on hearing the word Muzuri (good, success), a faint smile filtered through the waves of his beard. My sons were particularly interested in Juma and Samuel, being roughly the same age. That evening, the older sprout asked if I had cured Juma and I told him that I had operated on him. That seemed to satisfy him. We had other more immediate successes: a boy with a frontal osteoma which we treated successfully with a makeshift coronal flap, several lid and facial cancers, a couple of nasal deformities and a sprinkling of lacrimal, eyelid and orbital cases. It is not gilding the lily too much to say that at the end of a successful day, all seemed well with the world. However, with our Western agendas, we were impatient: the

locals, patients and staff alike, were in no hurry. At the end of the day, those that had not been seen left smiling, only to return the following day without so much as a murmur or complaint. Hakuna matata (no problems) seemed the local dictum. When we saw a tourist with an eye problem, looking prosperous in his fluorescent tank top pulled tight over an epic paunch, we were reminded of the rarity of obesity in this part of the world. The only overweight Africans we saw were the politicians on TV and bank managers. Success has its price.

Lest one gets the impression that we just worked, I should tell you that we played even harder: the old town, beaches, game preserves, and friends, old and new. In the labyrinthine streets of the Arab old town, figures sit in every doorway, shadows spilling out into the night. Arab, Indian, African and Western music fills the humid air punctuated with loud laughter. Women, black-hooded in the total mystery of their buibui shimmer by shyly with darting glances, as if suspicious they were being followed. Part of the usual denigration of Africa is the assertion that it has no architecture beyond the temporary throwing up of huts. Yet, the old town offers evidence of the complexity and skills of its ancestors, for the mosques are the last echoes of the first ziggurats.

It would have been remiss of us not take advantage of the visually delicious spectacle that is the African Savannah, what with the older shrimp being a great lover of the animal kingdom and all. We went on a three-day Safari (Arab word meaning voyage) and explored Karen Blixen's beloved Africa. We bucketed along potholed roads at a speed of knots leaving all the rear passengers with Africa-sized bruises on their

derrieres. We saw all the big game; at one point an enormous male elephant, stood in the middle of the road and stared at us, his ears flapping, tusks held up proudly. He seemed to be defiant, and quite rightly so. After all, we were the intruders.

The magic of these safaris is that they give you the time to become properly acquainted with East Africa's stunning visage and its intimate secrets. Visitors fall under the sway of Africa's breathtaking beauty. Few experiences can replace the visceral excitement of standing amidst a herd of resting elephants, being in on "the kill" with a pride of hungry lions (a cheetah in our case), seeing thousands of the zebras, wildebeest, gazelles, watching the elegant giraffes, or making eye contact with the King of the jungle, as we were fortunate enough to do.

The sight of untrammeled plains

rimmed with volcanoes and carpeted with thousands of antelope and wildebeest move the hearts of rogues as well as romantics. All three squirts, romantics every one of them, went "Cool" in unison at the sight of the majestic lions. As strong a vote of approval as you will ever get from them.

Those long, still moments when the engine is turned off and the real life of the animals is going on around you soak into the depths of your consciousness; so that many years from now your inner self will still feel the deep, warm strength of Africa, setting the mind's nerves tingling with the memory of Nature's richest canvas.

We had planned on climbing the magnificent Mt. Kilimanjaro, but time restricted us to admiring the mountain crowning the plains of the savannah from a distance. Few mountains in the world are as steeped in legend as this giant of Africa.

In the evening, sitting by the fireside under a tropical sky innocent of clouds, the sky bejeweled and blue as cobalt, we discussed politics, talked to friends and families and rued the changes that were threatening this splendid country.

It is a truism that people make a place. At first blush, all Kenyans may seem the same. But the people along the coast are a jolly lot, given to robust collegiality. Greetings are of great importance here. Before starting a conversation, speakers usually shake hands and share at least three greetings: for example, Habari gani, bwana (What news, sir?), and the person may respond Nzuri, Hujambo? (Well, how are you?) then, Sijambo (I'm fine). The greetings are decorated with much nodding, gesturing and lingering handshakes, which can stretch to several minutes if the sun is shining and there is nothing pressing to do, which is generally the case. Only then does conversation begin. Laughter is a dominant leitmotif of everyday conversation. Rarely is a conversation carried out without smiles and frequently outright hilarity. It is infectious; Neel took to it like a duck to water and soon, he was waving and smiling at everyone.

The Eastern Coast of Africa away from the towns is a laconic, largely rural area where life is still very pedestrian. If you want plum hotels with a groovy nightlife and fast food, sun-beds and umbrellas, if you want the chic, showy, easy, organized, pampered and familiar life (and why shouldn't you?), this is not for you. If on the other hand, you want to stay in languorous villages drenched in vivid Swahili way of life little changed over the last 800 years, if you want to immerse yourself in a lazy but invigorating unique culture

that will not give in to the fast lane of the 20th century, where every sentence seems to end with a lazy infectious laugh, then you have come to Shangri-La. Where the sand looks like a perfect white carpet, for mile after drowsy mile, where the nearest soul is actually a mile or so down the beach, where you can eat seafood dragged in from the ocean before your eyes. We stayed right on the beach under the swishing leaves of the tall coconut trees. We were told to be careful as just the week before a visitor had been killed by a falling coconut! That kind of danger we can handle. The sea is so blue it almost hurts the eyes. Except for the susurration of waves and the gentle breeze, a golden silence fills the space between the sea and the sky. Life could be dandy: life could be a beach.

At one beach hotel where we stayed for

a night, Club-Med type activities were thrust upon the guests; aqua Tae-Bo, and the like. My sons, both chips off the old block, would rather take ballet lessons than endure the hideous embarrassment of prancing around Tae-Bo-style: we ducked out before the MC could rope us in and escaped to the white expanses of Indian Ocean sands. We chased crabs, kicked sand, and talked of this, that and everything in between. Sheer bliss. In the afternoon, we sipped a heady mixture of mango juice and passion juice- shaken, of course, not stirred.

The old hotels along the coast are a dazzle of crystal and white-washed buildings, waiters in gleaming white with elbow-length gloves, summoning visions of colonial Africa, White Mischief, cocktails at seven, what, what. We walked in the footsteps of history by exploring the very beach where Vasco da Gama landed in 1498. I turned my ear towards the gentle play of sea on sand, listening for the galley-loads of Portuguese and Arabs reaching journey's end. If you listen carefully, you can still hear them. As we drifted along a warm, soft, sepia sea-breeze in an Arab dhow (ancient sailboat) sails silent as owls, the sweetness of temporarily leaving the machine age enveloped us. The dhows that have been plowing the waters since time immemorial, will still be sailing down the coast when the last iron ship has foundered and the last drop of oil has burned. When you swim near the coral reef, the fish alone jostle you as you watch them, and they you, in the 83 degree Indian Ocean. The sun set, leaving a last explosion of light along the Ocean's rim; the town scarlet, the sky salmon, the earth blood. It was the drunken dusk of a tropical paradise. You could see why wine was forbidden to Muslims.

Paradise has its problem, though. Typical Kenyan's earn only some $750 annually, according to World Bank statistics. There are the rich, of course, and the chasm between the haves and the have-nots is huge. The squalid village scenes, the unending repetition of rickety hovels and scabrous legs is heart-wrenching.

Towards the end of our stay, I frequently noted the two boys discussing events in conspirational whispers. Finally, the older shrub came up with the source of the heated debates. "Daddy," he began, with a sheepish grin, "you have a job here just like home. Can't we stay here forever?" "You do realize there will be no TV or your toys?" "No problem," he said. "And you will have to come to work with me whenever I say." "Hacuna matata."

"And they do twice as much homework as they do back home." "Okay," they said with big grins, a slight hesitation being the only betrayal that this wasn't the best news in the world. How do you explain to them that one has to make a living? Or that there are patients back home I enjoy treating as much as the ones here? Or that tax day was just around the corner? I settled for hugs all round. When in doubt, hug.

Some weeks after I returned, I got a message from my colleague in Africa: Juma's pressure was high again although not as bad as before. But his vision had deteriorated. Of course I knew what that meant. There was little vision to deteriorate and they were being kind in their correspondence. That evening, as I watched my two boys wrestling with each other and giggling over small amusements, I imagined Juma and Samuel with their unanimated faces and scared eyes. I couldn't imagine them giggling and wrestling. All was certainly not well with the world; "slings and arrows of outrageous fortune" came to mind. I hesitated to tell the boys of the calamity but felt it was necessary for them to experience the successes as well as the failures, dismal as they may be. To the terrible news, all my son had to say was, "But you can operate on him next time and get him better." Innocence conquers all. As she said, "This is most unfair."

And why should two boys make such a deep impression when one has seen many more, with perhaps more serious conditions? In fact, on the very day we operated on them, March 24, NATO dropped the first of many bombs on Kosovo, affecting tens of thousands, many fatally. It may be that they are children, or that they look like my two little urchins, or that it could all be prevented, or the haunting look of fear in their otherwise blank eyes, or the knowledge that they have a lifetime of darkness ahead, or maybe it is just because. Sadly, these memories do not fade. I still remember the banshee wail of a young boy, "Baba ame kufa!" (My father is dead), pounding his head on the wall, tears streaming down his face, on hearing that his dad had died during surgery. I was nine years old at the time. I remember it like it was yesterday.

I have rambled on a bit. But much has been left unsaid. Proust once wrote a whole book based on a dream and I could just as easily do the same (without the Proustian flair, I fear) around these two weeks. "How was Africa?" Well, now you know a little of how it really was.

105

There may be juicier experiences in life, but this trip came as close to taking the biscuit as any. I had the good fortune of the company of my youngest brother, I laughed once again with my best friend from when I was 12 years old, and made more friends, some among the delightful patients. My wife also was thoroughly relaxed. The kids, of course made the real difference and made me look at events and people through their eyes. In them, this memorable experience has germinated a lively interest in everything African. A splendid trip. And to all of you, I have only one thing to say: Polé, polé, sasa."

Focus Feature, Moran Eye Center
Used by permission of the author

MR. WARREN

Charlotte Freeman
Retired Drama Teacher

My goal in High School was to 'fit in.' As the daughter of a semi-invalid, former coal miner, I was brought up in a tiny mining camp. I had to ride a bus twelve miles to school. Skinny, awkward and nervously boisterous, I was determined to hang out with the 'right crowd.' These were children of doctors, lawyers, businessman and the like. They were the Student Council, members of all the foreign language clubs, the Pep Club, the Forensic team and the Thespian Society.

Thespian Society! Therein began my trouble. I knew I had what it took to be onstage. I had just not reckoned with the drama coach, Mr. Hutchinson. He was over six feet tall, over three hundred pounds and coach of our football team. So how did he ever get to be a drama coach?

I guess it was due to his very loud voice. Nevertheless, in a classroom filled with the 'right kids', I felt I was in my element. That was until the second week of school when Coach gave the assignment to design a floor plan for a play. We were to draw a 'rear elevation' listing the parts of each flat.

Flat!!?? Rear elevation!!?? Was he speaking Shakespeare or Greek? But my friend Dorothy, whom I revered, spoke for the entire class when she said, "Sure we can do that. When do you want it turned in?" At first I was hoping she was speaking for us to work together and turn in the assignment collectively. That was not the case. Rather than speak up and display my elevated sense of ignorance, I sat mutely and nodded agreement. That evening I went to my father in tears.

107

"Daddy, what am I going to do? He, meaning the Coach, is so demanding! He's . . . he's so loud. He isn't reasonable . . . he asks too much."

At this point daddy interjected, "Just what exactly does he want you to do?"

"He wants us to design a set and label the parts of the flats and I don't even know what a flat is . . . and what's more, neither do the other kids, except for Dorothy and Mike and Nick and Karen Lou. Well, at any rate, there are a lot of us who don't know what he's talking about and I don't want to fail. I want out of the class!"

Now my father who loved me more than life itself, put his arms around me and said not to worry; he'd figure it all out. So I headed off to bed.

The next day was school as usual. After lunch we had Forensics class. I wasn't exactly the best debater, but that didn't matter. The 'right kids' were in there and that's where I wanted to be also. We were all working in our teams looking for the best quotation to outwit our opponents. It took me by surprise when Mr. Warren quietly called me up and asked me to step outside into the hall. "Do you want to tell me what's going on, Miss Smith?" he asked looking straight into my very soul.

"I'm not sure. Pat and I are having a little trouble finding material good enough to beat Val and Mike; but other than that, nothing is wrong." I said this perhaps a bit too forcefully, not fully understanding to what he was alluding.

"This has nothing to do with debate. This has to with your acting class Coach Cunningham and your father."

"My father!?"

108

"Your father." Silence! "Your father who came to school today during lunch hour and spoke with the principal saying the Acting Coach could use some coaching himself because he had assumed that all of you understood his assignment, but obviously not all of you did."

Much more quietly I breathed, "My father . . . ?"

"Yup! He also said you want out of the class. Is that correct?"

"Well," I blurted, now close to tears, "he is so loud and he acts as if we all know what he's talking about and we don't and I don't want to look stupid, so it will just be easier if I transfer out."

Now the silence nearly burst my eardrums. For an interminable long moment he stared at me, measuring me from wind-disheveled hair to my scuffed oxfords. "I knew you were a lot of things, Miss Smith, but I never knew you were a quitter." The finality of his words struck me with such force I nearly reeled from the pain.

"I'm not a quitter," I whispered, with the most conviction I could muster.

"Then prove it." He waited a moment; then we discussed that which I had not been able to tell the other teacher. We worked out a viable solution. I saved face and stayed in the acting class.

I write this partly to say that if Mr. Warren had been a music teacher, I would be part of his 'Opus.' I went on to become a Teacher and Director of Theater. I, too, took many students out in the hall for 'a chat.' If I can hope for anything, I would hope that I have been a sentinel for at least one of my students as Neil Warren was for me.

109

Bridget Shaughnessy
Cryptographer

*S*everal years ago I had a good friend with whom I believed I had much in common. We had grown up in the same area, married, and had children of similar ages. We enjoyed each other's company, going walking or driving together when we could.

Then a tragedy happened. My friend's oldest son did something that was morally quite seriously wrong. My husband's position required that he be the one to discipline the young man. I remember a meeting in my home when my friend was incensed that her son was called to account. She flew into a rage and all but physically attacked my husband, screaming blame and abuse at him and demanding that the whole matter be ignored.

Of course that was impossible. It was serious, and other people had suffered as a result. And it was not a private thing. My husband was in a difficult position, but in spite of criticism, blame and unpleasantness, he stuck to his determination to be fair to everyone.

In the time that followed I could see that it made him very miserable, as it did me, although the young man himself readily admitted his part and accepted the outcome.

Our whole small community was torn by it, and I lost a friend I had valued. We are pleasant enough to each other now, but we no longer do anything together. She has not forgiven me because I did not take her back when I believed she was wrong.

I could understand her deep love for her son and the pain at knowing he would lose opportunities because of what he had done. But my husband's action showed me that the best love is that which sees a person honestly, the strengths and weaknesses, the successes and failures, and addresses them all. It can hurt at the time, but denial hurts more in the end. If we close our eyes to what is uncomfortable, then we leave deceit and unresolved wounds, and sooner or later someone else with their eyes open has to come along and clean up the mess.

My husband's quiet determination, at the right time, was far better for the young man than his mother's violent and blind defense would have been. I hated the whole experience, and the cost, but he changed my understanding of real kindness, and I have tried to live up to the difference.

I started out in the oil industry in the late '70s, working on the oil rigs in the North Sea. In the very early '80s I met Bobby Rae Toney. He was a typical Texan from the South, tall, broad shouldered and he spoke with a slow drawl. He was Project Manager, and I was responsible for document control, which included all the drawings, specifications and certifications.

I found it difficult on the oil rigs at first. It was an environment completely alien to me, and of course potentially dangerous. I was something of a loner, particularly where work was concerned, and here was I now living on a platform in the North Sea having to co-operate closely with men, mostly engineers of one sort or another, college graduates, and some pretty arrogant, expecting me to read their minds from a half sentence of demands or in-

112

structions. Needless to say, at times I failed.

Even though he was busy, Bobby Rae always made time to explain things to me, teaching me how to read the diagrams and learn each man's job and his needs so I could understand what he required of me. He told me if I was in doubt always to ask, not only the facts but the reasons behind them.

Gradually he taught me instead of looking inward with my work, to look outward, to read the men's requirements and understand them individually, to realize that a mistake of a line or figure could endanger not only valuable equipment but possibly someone's life. I had never seen our interdependence before, or worried about being part of the team, but before long I began to value the link. Experience by experience I not only became trustworthy, knowing I had to be 100% right in what I gave them, but I learned to trust them also. Bobby Rae taught me a whole new way of looking at work, of being part of a larger whole, a part that must be totally reliable. Never give your word unless you can keep it, but once you give it you are bound. You must do what you have said you will. Other men have trusted you. That is something of profound value and you must never betray it.

I still think of Bobby Rae with a smile, friendship and gratitude.

As a young man, I was the shyest individual you could imagine. I would never get on a bus or train if it was more than half full and would never run to catch a bus, but would rather walk home from work, cinema or pub.

Being such an introvert it was a trial to meet new people or to speak out when in a group (which I really hated) so I tended to spend a lot of time on my own. Until an old school friend invited me to a meeting in London (which was about thirty miles away) and I met a man who was known as Harvey. This man had an amazing effect on my life!

Within six weeks he had me running along the center aisle of the Conoult rooms in London, which held anywhere between 300–1000 people, leaping on to the stage to do a 15 minute presentation on a cleaning product and then introduce Harvey for the closeout in a pyramid selling organization.

In private I remember Harvey to be a quiet, small and unassuming man, but in public he was a giant, bubbling confidence, saying all the right things, full of desire to succeed and giving that same desire to almost every person that heard him.

In a short time with help from Harvey, I was on top of my own pyramid with a large organization under me. When the bubble burst it left me owing the bank 1.600.00£ and that was over thirty years ago. The experiences with this very clever con man were both good and bad. They left me with many principles that have held me in good stead over the years, some of which I list below.

1. The things you hate to do the most. Do them first and do them well.

2. If you say you are going to do something you do it.

3. Be very careful where you place your trust.

When I was about 20 years old I managed to get some work as a laborer with an established and experienced builder. We were helping to renovate a 600-year-old Dutch barn, and one of the things we had to do was remove the bricks from under the timber part of the structure and clean off the 600-year-old cement. It was very dirty, boring work. The guy I was working for convinced me to do the best job I could. When the work was finished I was able to see that without the bricks as clean as we got them the whole barn would have looked like we hadn't cared about the project and it would have looked horrible.

It made me realize that when doing any job it isn't just the big things that count but also the small "unimportant" things that make it worth doing.

115

Vanessa Nelson
Teacher

*A*s I approach the conclusion of my years on earth, reflection is a constant element which brings me happiness and content. Though I have not done anything wonderful for which I will be immortalized, I have managed to leave a small influence on those who follow me. Perhaps I have been a small signal light for some, but what astounds me is the amazing influence that others have had on my life. They were sentinels along the way who shaped me and led me.

I am a teacher by nature, and by heart, loving few things more than being in my classroom with a group of happy children. Yet, after thirty eight years, it was a child who really taught me the most important lesson in my professional life. Russell, my grandson, was born in 1994, with severe problems. He was hydrocephalic, and soon underwent an operation to put a shunt into his small head so that spinal fluid would not fill the cranial cavity and result in his death. After nearly a month in intensive care, he finally came home and had to be tube fed.

His development certainly was not normal and he eventually was diagnosed with Coffin-Lowery Syndrome, a form of mental retardation. I had always taught GIFTED children in school. I was used to dealing with children whose brains could absorb as fast as mine could output. That was in sharp contrast to Russell who did not even learn to walk until about two and one-half. But there he was, a constant, in my life. Russell's father was killed in an accident prior to his birth, so his mother, sister, and Russell came to live with us. At age nine he is not yet fully diaper trained and can say the alphabet, but only recognizes a few letters.

116

When he was little I'd often tell people (because he could not speak) that he communicated in the pure language of Adam and that I had not learned it yet. Perhaps my words, spoken in jest, are true. At any rate, he slowly learned to speak which was a great blessing. He now has the mind of a three-year-old, but the soft heart of one who has lived at the side of God. His love knows no bounds and his forgiveness when we are impatient with him is beyond my comprehension. It is always," I'm sorry grandma," with tears running down his tiny cheeks.

What a contrast he made in my life with the quick-learning, able, and eager students I taught. Once when he was about two, just learning to walk, he somehow broke his leg—we never did find out what happened. No one knew why he was crying so hard. I gave him a bath having no idea that the leg was broken. He gave me no indication of where the pain was. When I took him out of the tub and tried to have him stand, I saw that little foot recoil in pain, and only then rushed him to the hospital. I was so foolish and he suffered because of me. I can still see him with that tiny blue cast on his little leg, trying to move his red push car across the floor. He had just taken a few steps on his own and now the process again had to wait.

How much that little boy taught me about patience, and about understanding individual differences. We can't all run the race at the same speed and finish at the same time, but I feel blessed that Russell can at least run. He'll never win a race, but he can run. I see many who cannot stand, or move, and my eyes often well with tears. "There, but for the will of God, go I," is the phrase which haunts my mind. I notice with great pain that others stare at him with strange wondering eyes, and I know that children in their often cruel ways laugh at him. That stabs like a knife, and yet I can do little to help him with this human unkindness he must endure his whole life. He does not understand when things, which we perceive he could damage, are taken away from him by his big sister, and so his tears flow. He loves cars, but will never drive one. He loves books, but will probably never read one on his own.

It has been said, "A mind to do thinking, two hands and two eyes is all the equipment God gives to the wise." Who knows what wisdom lies behind those soft eyes. Now in my classroom when I'm helping Sami who is about two years behind in her skills, and who has difficulty understanding, I think of my own dear little

Russ, and I take more time to help, not expecting great achievement from all, but hoping for slow progress. I can't bear to think of life without that dear little boy. In his infinite wisdom, he has taught me to be more wise and more thoughtful. Often my impatience shows, and later I pray for God to give me more of that elusive quality. I have a long way to go in my development of that skill, much further than he has to go with his alphabet.

It is my own personal belief that one day Russell will possess a bright, clear mind, and a body which will do his bidding, but that time is in the life beyond this. He has been one of my sentinels here on earth, and his life will shine brighter still in the kinder, and more understanding world to come.

Doris S. Platt
Compiler

I have always been grateful for the teachers in my life . . . for the giants among us, giants found in the most unexpected places . . . for people who swim in certainty and know who they are, and for people trying to find out. And the gifts, always the gifts. Aware that I like both the security of long-range planning and the exhilarating spontaneity of the moment, a friend asked if I would accompany her on an impromptu four-day research trip to California. The excursion was a mere two and a half weeks before Christmas, but that only added to the sense of adventure. Feeling like teenagers skipping school, we flew to San Francisco, rented a car, and drove north along the California coast. Intermittent rain did not prevent our taking notes and photographs along the way. Darkness found us at Jenner's Inn. On a walk early the next morning, we discovered that the nearby Russian River had overflowed its banks. An odd assortment of flotsam and jetsam was moving on its roiling, muddy surface. It was a wild, lonely scene. Turning away from the river, we saw a man walking towards us and, for the briefest of moments, felt a sense of unease. Even from a distance, my friend and I both knew there was something different about him. We exchanged greetings, and our impression was confirmed. He did indeed have some mental challenges. The man proudly informed us that he was on his way to clear the debris from the river where it met the sea. A native of the area, he said he had been doing this for years. Given the size of the tree trunks floating in the water, we wondered how his task could be accomplished but wished him well. Before he continued on his way, he calmly stated, "Now you can say you've met someone." Sometimes I remember his parting words and wonder how many of us know as much. His words were the gift I took away with me.

119

Sharon Dayton
Wilderness Guide / Outfitter

At nineteen years of age I was working my first year as a professional guide for an established outfitter. Although I had hunted six years with relatives out of a family camp in an adjacent area, this land was unfamiliar and without outstanding landmarks. It was useful and reassuring to join another longtime guide on a days hunt.

Horses were saddled and hunters breakfasted in the pre-light dawn, rifles checked and scabbarded, lunches secured in saddlebags, hunters mounted led off and started down the trail as light was breaking. The day's destination was seven miles away in the Bridger Teton National Forest. From our camp at the edge of Big Park our horses carried us through timbered ridges and vast plateaued forestlands towards Devils Hole. Devil's Hole drops suddenly to what seems the depth of the earth—a great grassy bowl with patches of brush and trees descending down the ridge.

It was there we discovered our quarry, massive yellow-bodied elk grazing the open sides. Our position allowed us to see them—glass them—and evaluate them as trophies, but open land between them and us made successful stalking impossible. The distance made firing with successful impact chancy. Frustrated with that dilemma we traveled on to other areas as the sun moved across the October sky. But being in the right place at the right time wasn't happening on this day and as evening approached it was time to turn our mounts towards camp. Half a mile toward camp we saw movement on a distant hill and closer inspection confirmed our impression that these were the game we sought. Turning our horses over to the head guide—Don—we gathered rifles, skinning knives, cartridges and began a descent into the canyon. The sun was down now but there was still shooting light as we climbed the opposite hill—weaving our way up the elevation.

Using patches of timber to shield our approach and stepping carefully we moved toward our quarry trying to come within shooting range without spooking and driving the elk into the timber. Darkness was approaching when good opportunity presented itself and I directed my hunters to fire at their targets.

Fortunately the range was reasonable —their firing accurate—and two animals dropped to be claimed and tagged. As hunters say "and then the work begins" with huge animals to be field dressed—now in the darkness. It was a process that took two hours in dark and unfamiliar country using flashlights for light. Finally the job completed- the game propped for cooling- it was time to consider return to camp—but which way in total darkness—no sounds— no hint of direction—no knowledge of camp direction—uneasiness—concern—and then a spot of light to focus on—a long way off. It was a flickering light that promised warmth and hope—that one fire on a distant ridge—a place to go to. After descending to the canyon depth and what seemed like endless climbing the light was once again in view and there was the lead guide with the bonfire and horses waiting to show me the way home.

✳ ✳ ✳

Sharon Dayton has hunted the land of the Bridger Teton Forest for 55 years—guided and outfitted for more than 40 years, putting on about 70,000 miles on horseback.

From Ego To Humility

Bob Bedore
Actor

As an actor for nearly twenty five years, I've lived under the pretense that an ego is not only a byproduct of acting, but it's also your greatest defense mechanism and motivator. I've strived to be the best I can because I felt I owed it to the audience; they deserve to see the best person in my part, and if I wasn't the best, I shouldn't be there.

Or so I thought until I had the privilege to act along side a man who not only changed much of my life, but became one of my very best friends.

Mike Westenskow was not only an actor of great talent, but one blessed with a rare eye for seeing the best in everyone. Mike shared that eye with me one day and that vision changed the way I saw the world.

I was involved in a community theater show and knew that my "talent" was far superior to the rest of the cast, many doing a show for the first time in their lives. I worked hard and harder to lift the show. At times I felt like I was carrying the cast on my shoulders and dragging them along. I knew I was giving the crowd a fine show and felt good about it.

But Mike saw it differently. He told me how I had ruined the show with my acting. I was shocked. I had put everything into the show, and I told him as much. He agreed, I had worked hard, and yes, he could see my ability on the stage. But Mike told me that by doing this I had made the others around me look worse. I had taken away their opportunity to experience the true love of the performance. I had also taken the audience out of the show because there was no longer a feeling of continuity on stage, but rather one person running his own show.

I thought about this for a moment and realized how right he was. I thought back to all the times I'd watched Mike perform with "lesser" actors and just how good he made them look. He had an incredible ability to bring his acting to the level of those around him, thus raising the performance as a whole.

Mike treated everyone as if they were the best person he could have acting with him. It was wonderful to watch, and to be a part of it. He did the same thing in real life with all those around him. To this day I know of no one who came in contact with Mike that doesn't hold him in the highest regard.

Odd to think that in an industry full of egos and glory hounds, the best I ever knew was the most humble. Sadly a car accident took Mike's life and with it the chance for him to touch others with his ability.

The world lost one of the few people who saw everyone as a genius—and I lost a friend.

I'm still a long way from Mike and his vision of the world, but with each remembrance of him and his humility, I like to think that I draw a little closer. It would be wonderful if we saw each other as Mike did; I just wish I had seen him one last time.

Harry Nash
Senior Partner, Accounting Firm

"Oi 'Arry, get us the noospapers—Mirror and Sportin' life."

How well I remember those words uttered by a great grizzly bear of a man during my junior school summer holidays. He would be standing by his gate at No. 9 wearing, as was the "style" for that time, his trousers, no shirt, and suspenders just over his vest. Very late 1940s Stamford Hill style!

I remember during those days, looking out of my bedroom window around 8:30 a.m. waiting until I could see him. I would then go downstairs, having had my breakfast, and tell my mother that I was going to the local corner shop to buy a comic book. Knowing he was there, I would walk past his house, albeit on the other side of the road.

I lived at No. 24, and as I said, he lived at No. 9. As I approached perhaps No. 16, diagonally opposite No. 9 I would wait for those gruff Cockney tones asking me to buy him the newspapers. Why did I always pray that he would stop me? Because he always gave me 6d (2 1/2 p now) for my troubles. That 6d was a fortune in 1947/1948 for an eight year-old. In a good week I would "earn" maybe two shillings, enough for a visit to the cinema and an ice cream with some change for a comic or a float to carry me through the week.

Given that my pocket money was 6d per week and the cinema was 9d you can see why I really liked Mr. Bloomfield. (In those days everyone who was not family, but a friend of one's parents, was Mr. . . . never ever to be called by a scruffy eight year old by first name.)

Mr. Bloomfield was in fact Joe Bloom-

124

field, a well-known Jewish light heavyweight boxer during the 1930s (not as successful as his brother Jack, who I think fought for the British heavyweight title around the same time). Joe had married Esther, a non Jew, who eventually converted to Judaism so that her oldest daughter could marry in an Orthodox synagogue. By the time I knew him he had long finished boxing and was, as far as I can remember, employed at Stamford Bridge dog track, putting out the stalls for the bookmakers. (That is what I heard anyway.)

I had a special "in" with him because:

1. My late father, a boxing fan, knew him from the old East End days and,

2. His youngest daughter Janice was my sister's best friend.

He never treated me like a little boy. While not discussing world politics with me (I very much doubt either of us could have done so anyway) he treated me as a young adult and was not patronizing in any shape or form. When I passed my entrance exam for the local grammar school, at age 11, it was as of his own son had passed. He knew that I liked boxing and used to spar with me in his garden.

Always smiling, always cheerful, he was loved by one and all. I can see him, as I said before, in the summer without his shirt, suspenders over his vest, and in the winter months wearing a long overcoat, never buttoned up, and a jacket, also unbuttoned and his shirt without a tie. This was his dress through the winter months. I never ever remember seeing him with a tie or with his jacket or overcoat buttoned up. In fact the only time I remember ever seeing him wearing a suit was at his oldest daughter's wedding.

He was loved by his family and was devoted to them. I think that Joe was the original rough diamond and when I heard that he had died I cried for the first time in my life. I was around seventeen years old.

He was generous to the point of being easy pickings for us kids and I'm not amazed that I still remember him vividly. As I grew older, I realized that we do not have to talk "posh" nor wear expensive designer suits to have the heart, to be kind or as it is said in Yiddish to be a "mensch."

Mr. Bloomfield epitomized all the best traits of humanity and now I realize that he was not necessarily accepted by the local glitterati at that time because of his background i.e. a boxer, marrying a lady who was not of the "faith" (she, too, was a beautifully kind lady) and did not dress a-la-mode.

A simple man in that he was not able to have been academically educated he was someone, even at the age of eight, I wanted to pass the time of day with.

Dr. Kick

By Sakasem Kanthawong,
Three-time Muay Thai World Champion
As told to Julie Adams

We had no TV. The first time I heard about him, about Apidit, was on the radio. I was maybe nine, maybe ten years old. They called him "Jumtak," that means "Dr. Kick." He would fight every month, sometimes two times a month. They would get so excited, talking about his fights on the radio. "Apidit, kick! Kick! Kick!" He would kick fast, five fast kicks, Bam! Bam! Bam! Knockout! They would say, "He broke his opponent's leg! He broke the arm! A knockout!" They would say, "Jumtak Bangnukkrac is the champion!"

It was my dream to train like him, to be like him. He was a famous Muay Thai fighter. That's what I wanted to be. People knew who he was; everyone knew who he

was. I wanted them to know who I was, too.

That's how he first changed my life, and he didn't even know me. I was bad before I heard of Apidit. In school, I was in fights all the time. I had seven brothers. We beat up everyone. We were a gang. We were mean. Apidit saved my life. My life changed when I heard about his fights.

When I was twelve, I started to fight Muay Thai. After about five years, I had beaten everyone in Chaingmai (my hometown). There was no one left to fight. I was the best, so I moved to Bangkok to train at Fairtex (a world-renowned Thai boxing training camp). The day I arrived, Apidit arrived, too! It was my first day to train; it was his first day as a trainer there; so two dreams came true for me, to train at

127

Fairtex, and to train with Apidit.

He liked me from the very first day. He liked my power. I always trained hard, like I was going to fight. Kick the bag, hard! That first day, he told Philip Wong, the owner of Fairtex, that he wanted to train me. I was seventeen; he was thirty-five. I remember that every day after training, I had to take him to the taxi stand on my bike. He took a taxi to his home every night. He rode on the back of my bike, through Bangkok every day. I found out what a good person he was. Not just a good fighter, a good person. I wanted to be like him, that's how he changed my life. Nobody knew me. Everybody knew him. I wanted to be like him—a good fighter, a good person. Mean in the ring, good on the street.

Now Apidit is sixty-five years old, and he's still quick, smart. He still fights and he still teaches techniques to the fighters. Because of him I'm good fighter, and a good trainer. I told him one time, "When I was younger you saved my life. I used to fight all the time, and always got in fights in school. But I stopped when I heard your fights." Everyone knows him still. But now, everyone knows me also.

✳ ✳ ✳

Sakasem "The Punisher" Kanthawong is a three-time world champion in Muay Thai, with over 225 professional fights. He has never been knocked out. With a fighting history that spans thirty-five years, Sakasem is a well-respected fighter and trainer in both the United States and Thailand.

Bryan Swan
Student, Mechanical Engineering

I truly believe that there are major turning points every so often in one's life. One of the most major turning points happened when I was very young. I can only imagine how different things would be right now if it hadn't been for a particular person that actually showed a little faith in me.

The pertinent story begins when I entered elementary school. I was the second youngest of seven children, or the second forgotten child of seven. My two oldest sisters are Twins that excelled in everything they even thought about doing. My oldest brother was one of the coolest brothers one could have, but he's also the oldest son. His grades were not as good as those of our sisters, but he could do anything he put his mind to. Then there is another sister, the youngest daughter, daddy's girl, and all-around perfect child. Then my

older brother, the first forgotten. He was really intelligent, but just didn't apply himself to anything. He didn't play competitive sports like the rest of us, didn't get good grades, but scored rather high on the ACT test on his first try. He just didn't seem to care. Then I came. And last, but not least, my little brother. The youngest son, the cute one. He was that the baby of the family and took up most of everybody's attention.

I seemed to do okay in kindergarten, but school became hard for me starting in the first grade. I couldn't seem to pick up on reading as well as the other kids, nor pass my +4's on the timed math quizzes. I remember sitting in parent-teacher conferences and listening to my teacher talk to my mother about how I wasn't as smart as the other children. She talked to my mother as if I wasn't even there and as if I

129

couldn't understand what she was talking about. Maybe I couldn't understand everything, but I understood what was going on. I was finding out that I was stupid. I was put in the lowest level of the reading classes and had to read extra books at home to give me additional practice. I wasn't good enough. I just wasn't good enough.

I had a nice teacher in the second grade, but it was the same story. My mother and I would go to see the teacher for these parent-teacher conferences and get a new list of things I needed to improve on. I remember hating to have to sit and read more "I am Sam . . ." books and hating how stupid and simple the stories were while my friends were out playing. I just wasn't good enough at reading. I could tell that my parents started to believe that I wasn't as smart as the other children in the way they talked to me. They would encourage and help me, but there was just that feeling of acceptance of my lack of ability in their attitudes towards me. The scary thing for me is that I started to believe it. I accepted the fact that I wasn't smart. I couldn't figure things out on my own. I was stupid.

The third grade is when everything changed. I was in Mrs. Lyons's class. She was a fairly new teacher in my elementary school and had a different attitude about her than the other teachers. She talked to us as if we were people. There was a time when I had missed school because I had broken my ribs at recess and when I came back she personally took the time to show me how to write letters in cursive that we had learned while I was gone instead of telling me to have my parents help me. She told me that I was doing very well and what a good student I was. I remember standing there in shock not knowing how to react. I thanked her for the complement, like my mother had taught me, and ran home to tell her even though I was in great pain.

The very moment that the change took place was in another parent-teacher conference between my mother and Mrs. Lyons. I sat there and listened to Mrs. Lyons tell my mother was a wonderful child I was and how thoughtful of other students. She talked about how well I was doing academ ically and also with reading. I watched my mother's expression change from a "what do I have to do now to help him," to a look of pride and gratitude. Mrs. Lyons talked to my mother as if I was the smartest student in her class and gave me reassuring looks as if I was. When she handed me my report card it showed the highest marks possible in every subject. I thought for sure that I was the smartest child in her class and maybe even the world.

From that point on I knew that I was smart enough to do anything asked of me. Whether or not I truly was as good a student as Mrs. Lyons said or not, it turned my whole attitude and the attitude of my parents towards me around. I wanted to live up to what Mrs. Lyons saw in me. I liked her version of me more than what I saw in myself up to that point.

I now believe she was inspired to say what she did and I can only imagine what I would be like she hadn't. I am a few classes short of graduating with a Bachelor's degree in mechanical engineering. It has been a long and rough road academically for me, but without the motivation from a third-grade teacher I would never have made it to this point in my life.

Thank you for everything, Mrs. Lyon!

131

Ibrahim Madany
Senior Vice President
Dearborn Federal Credit Union, ret.

My biggest regret is that I forgot the names, and therefore lost contact with, two very fine professors that helped me to come to a college in the United States and changed the course of my life. I would love to see them and be able to thank them for their help.

I was fortunate to go to school at an American mission school in Aleppo, Syria. After finishing high school and two years of college, I was hired by the same school to be the assistant to the director of the boarding department. During the summer the one hundred fifty students from all over the country plus a few of the neighboring countries went home. A few of us teachers stayed at the boarding department.

During the summer of 1955 two American professors from the University of Michigan came to Syria to do Anthropology work and St. Simion in a nearby city and resided in our boarding department. I struck up a friendship with them and they discovered that I wanted to finish my education in the United States. I had submitted my application to a few universities without having much success. They offered to help me through their connection at the University of Michigan, which I accepted very gladly, even though I knew very little about the university except that it was in the Midwest.

Within a month they received an answer from the University advising them that they had referred my application and file to Eastern Michigan College seven miles from Ann Arbor so that could I could acclimate to life in United States at a smaller campus. At that time Eastern Michigan had about 3,500 students. Within a few weeks I received my acceptance.

I arrived at Eastern during the fall of 1956. I finished my undergraduate and master's degrees at Eastern. I became Senior Vice President of Dearborn Federal Credit Union, which was and is the largest in the Midwest. I married, had two daughters, five grandchildren, and am very happy and proud to be an American citizen in this wonderful free country.

Keith, Commitment, and the Zen of Scuba Diving

John Blake
Financial Advisor / Master Scuba Diving Instructor

I am fortunate. At each of the major crossroads in my life—and there have been many—I have had an advisor or "sentinel" to help define my path. First and foremost were my parents, then spiritual advisers and teachers. Finally, there were professional associates, friends, and of course, my wife. As I write, there are faces and feelings associated with each, and the story of a major turning point where their example or influence guided my course and set me on the path that is my life today. When I say, "I am fortunate," I refer to the fact that the sentinels in my life pointed out what, in retrospect, I believe to have been a correct course for me. I have had access to thoughtful and intelligent people who cared enough about me to give me their best and most considered advice.

In Robert Frost's "The Road Not Taken," the traveler stands at the fork in the road and considers his options alone. In the end we wonder if the path that was taken was the right one for him. Does he regret the road not taken? We are only left with the ambivalent line, "and that has made all the difference." As I have come to those "yellow woods" in my life and stood at the forks in the road, it seems there has always been someone to consider my options with. "So what do you think about the road that is grassy and wants wear?" "Do you have any insights on that 'more worn path' that bends, just so, there in the undergrowth?"

Each gave me their considered opinion. Some had trodden the road before and knew the paths and their respective merits and pitfalls. I think oftentimes when people's lives go careening at breakneck speed toward, and sometimes over the precipice, it is because there was no reliable sentinel to say: "Slow down there. The road ahead is dangerous. The view is spectacular, but you want to make sure to take a right turn there—just after the big rock—and before the cliff." I was always counseled, warned, and encouraged. I was, and am, fortunate indeed.

Twelve years ago, I was a health care administrator and director of a Neurological Rehab Unit for a rehabilitation hospital owned by the largest "for profit" Hospital Corporation in the world. Today I run a financial planning firm and teach scuba diving on the side. The sentinel that stood at that fork in the road was, and is, a dear friend. I'll call him Keith—since that is his name and I don't think he would mind me using it.

I began my career in health-care as a Recreational Therapist. I counseled persons who had been catastrophically disabled by a spinal cord injury, dramatic brain injury, or stroke, on how to become a whole person again in a recreational context. I helped them to re-integrate back into the community, taught compensatory recreational skills, and helped design prostheses that aided them in achieving their

135

recreational goals despite their current disability.

Keith was a social worker on the spinal cord injury team. He had become disabled in a hunting accident at the age of 14, when he was shot in the back by a young friend, rendering him paraplegic. The term disabled, however, never really applied well to Keith. He is the most physically active person I know. His enthusiasm for a new challenge is contagious. We've been camping, boating and ice fishing together. I've watched him finish a marathon. He still hunts. He recently rode his arm powered bike across America (from Seattle to Washington D.C.), and represented the United States in the events at the 2002 Salt Lake City Winter Para Olympics—biathlon and cross-country skiing. He is raising a beautiful family. He is a leader in his church and a contributing member of his community.

Keith was the perfect social worker for our patients; he'd already been down the road. He was also the perfect teammate for me on our recreational adventures. The synergy was great. He could do better social work in the non-threatening environment of recreational activity, and I benefited from his insights on adapted to recreation. Our patients benefited most of all.

I remember once coming out of a wheelchair basketball practice with a group of young patients. Keith was playing on the team. We encouraged them to shoot a few shots and try to move around the court with the ball. Afterwards, we headed to the van for our return trip to the hospital. We emerged from the gym to darkness and a blinding snowstorm. The wheelchair ramp and rails were iced and covered with snow. Our patients parked outside the door in the snow and darkness with looks on their faces that said, "OK, what now?"

Keith came blasting out of the doors, bypassed the ramp and skipped down the short flight of stairs in his wheelchair, spun around and scooped up a handful of snow: "C'mon ya pansies, it's just a little snow," as he pelted the group with snowballs. A snowball war ensued. Once covered in snow from the fight, the ramp and snow-covered rails weren't so daunting. Everyone got to the van unaided. The outing was a success.

There were fishing expeditions, concerts, skiing trips, tennis outings. It was great work—fulfilling work; but it didn't pay well. I found myself with a young family trying to make ends meet and struggling. So I followed the money. I was offered a position in marketing and administration for a brain injury rehab company. After a year, I was offered the directors position at the hospital—big money, big pressure. Health care was changing. Mergers and acquisitions were a constant part of the landscape. Our referral sources began developing the own in-house rehab units and our hospital census was dropping. My job had me on the road constantly trying to develop new referral sources. They were endless meetings to develop programs that would give us a new competitive edge.

Keith and I talked many times during this period about the things we wanted to do with our lives, and the "good ole days" when we just worked with patients and helped them achieve their goals. Both of us

137

talked about leaving healthcare and pursuing other careers. Keith had been considering a change, and had talked to several high-tech recreational wheelchair manufacturers about getting sponsored to pursue his recreational pursuits while working for them as a factory rep. I had developed an interest in financial planning and was pursuing my credentialing in that area. I also wanted to write a book, take up scuba diving, and develop some mountain property owned by my family into a specialized resort, accessible to persons with disabilities. We were both comfortably uncomfortable. Comfortable with the money and a facade of security the hospital provided, uncomfortable in our lack of fulfillment brought by the changing professional landscape.

One day, as I was musing over some financial reports, Keith came wheeling into my office. He threw a sheet of paper on my desk, popped his wheelchair up on two wheels, spun around, and shot out never saying a word. I picked up the sheet. It read in bold letters:

"UNTIL ONE IS COMMITTED THERE IS HESITANCY"

At the time, I was not sure if he was telling me that he had made a decision to leave, or if he was telling me that I should follow my heart to pursue my own dreams. Regardless of the intent, it put me at a fork in the road again. And there was Keith and his enthusiastic sense of adventure, and his quote, saying, "Hey, quit biding your time! Get out of your rut!—That way looks good!"

Keith didn't just give me a quote that changed the direction and meaning of my life. I saw in him a man who was committed to important pursuits, and who daily lived by the spirit of those powerful words.

I left the hospital within six months. Keith followed his own course several months later. He now teaches Recreational Therapy at a major university. He is working on a Ph.D. and keeps his hands in healthcare as a part-time consultant and social worker for persons with spinal cord injuries.

I became a financial planner, a profession where I can help others to prepare for the future and even sometimes help them to extricate themselves from a financial boondoggle. It also gave me the freedom and time to pursue other interests. I learned to scuba dive; then I just kept going. It became a passion I wanted to share with others, so I became a scuba instructor, then a Master Scuba Diver Trainer. I've traveled more of the world than I ever expected as a result of my diving. My family now dives with me. I have made new friends and even new financial clients through my association with, and passion for, scuba diving. The novel is being written; developing the mountain property is still a dream for the future.

As a recreational therapist, I became a student of the works of Mihalyi Csikszentmihalyi. He developed the psychological model of "flow theory." In a nutshell, he said that we spend much of our lives searching for a particular experience that he termed "flow" because it was the word that was used most often by the subjects of his studies to describe the experience. When an individual finds an activity that they have great passion for, it is generally because the activity presents them with some element of challenge. When the challenge presented by the activity is greater than our ability to perform we experience anxiety. When our ability to perform far exceeds the challenge of the activity we experience boredom. Somewhere between and beyond boredom and anxiety is the experience of flow.

Flow experiences make us feel empowered and self affirmed. Like the adage that we can never "step twice in the same river" because it is constantly changing, flow is dynamic. And so we grow from competency to competency, changing, growing, becoming ever more skilled. Scuba diving has become my "flow activity." Whether challenging myself with a new environment or skill, or meeting the challenges posed by a new student who is struggling with their

own competency, the experience is very often flow producing. It re-affirms my sense of self. It is part of my identity now. It renews me.

Keith taught me that, as human beings, we need to be challenged-and, that in order to progress, we need to commit ourselves to new courses of action that have the capacity to produce those challenges in our own lives.

As human beings, we have a continual need to develop new competencies. I've witnessed my friend go through physical pain and financial risk to reach a goal. Sometimes we choose our course, sometimes it is chosen for us. Either way, our level of commitment to some major purpose is the key to whether we succeed or fail. I believe it was Napoleon Hill who said "when a man desires a thing so deeply that he's willing to stake his entire future on a single turn of the wheel in order to get it, he is sure to win."

Scuba diving has become a powerful metaphor for my life. There is some risk; you cannot be "sort of committed" to it without putting your life in danger. There are competencies to learn, risks to take, and work to do; but, if done right, the experience is powerful, worthwhile and fulfilling. You cannot be dishonest with water, nor can you teach natural laws of physics that govern the behavior of gases under pressure. Knowing those laws and subjecting yourself to them brings physical freedom that few people ever know.

I've witnessed many of the great wonders of the oceans of the world. By applying the same energy, passion, honesty and commitment to other aspects of my life, I am able to find fulfillment in my profession, with my family, and in my public life. Thanks, Keith, for setting an example, for standing at the fork in the road and knowing me well enough to point the way.

141

Timothy Webb
Literary Agency Bookkeeper

A number of years ago now I lived outside London, and commuted every day. I had never traveled beyond England. It took some effort on my part to decide that if I was to go to New York as requested by my, then, employer, I would first have to 'learn to fly' and enter the rest of the world on its terms.

I had corresponded with, and spoken to, my company's main American agent for many years but we had never met. I arrived in New York with great trepidation and certainty that, as in all the television and films I had seen, I would be mugged and shot on sight. The streets of Manhattan where unlike anything I had seen, buildings towering above me, well-named 'sky-scrapers.' Even the traffic policemen carried real guns!

Shortly after arriving safely at my hotel,

and resolving that I had already done enough and could stay in my room for the week (people could come to the hotel and meet me there), the phone rang and a friendly voice I knew asked whether I was free now and fancied a walk.

I did leave my room and was guided quite happily through Central Park along Broadway, around Times Square and into Greenwich Village, places which even I had heard of. Then we stopped for dinner at an obviously favorite restaurant. Later, we were joined by a couple of male friends of my guide. The place was unlike anywhere I had been before. The dress, the jewelry, the hairstyles and voices were cheerful, friendly but completely alien to me. I realized only then that I was in a totally different culture, and completely out of my depth.

I didn't really know what I expected to happen. The earth still revolved and I didn't stop breathing, and nothing awkward happened to me.

As with the World in general, New York specifically and with my new acquaintances, at that time my preconceived ideas, presumably learned from birth and fostered by parents, bore no relation to the actual experience I had.

I have now flown all over the world and have adjusted my preconceptions of people as well as places. No more snap judgments.

. . . met up again several times in New York and London over the years since. He will never know how he changed my thinking as, sadly, he died about a year ago and being English I would never been able to tell him anyway.

Pam Worley
Cabin Dweller/Dabbler in the Arts

For twenty-six years I've lived in the interior of Alaska, a transplant from the Mediterranean climate of Southern California. Just living day to day in a land where snow settles on the landscape in mid-September and sometimes lingers until May, sets up circumstances in which we all must look out for one another—to be without shelter or warm clothing can be a death sentence. One who lives here rarely forgets that life is fragile.

The indigenous people, who originally inhabited this place of extremes and now share it with the rest of us, are often relegated to second-class citizen status. In Fairbanks, many of these residents and visiting village people gather in small bars or bingo parlors sprinkled along two streets in the main part of town.

I work part-time in a gift shop on Cushman Street around the corner from various watering holes and gambling spots. By the time I close up, reconcile the cash register and re-stock; the majority of local workers have emptied out the parking lots. The sidewalks are sparsely populated, save a few folk passing by, some stumbling along the icy walkways, their balance impaired by an afternoon of drinking. Amidst this evening population, I have found myself on the receiving end of serendipitous acts of kindness and protection from those whose names I have yet to know. Some acts of caring are performed by sentinels I've never seen.

After realizing, one snowy evening, that my favorite ice scraper/snow brush (the one with the ergonomic handle, crisp metal edge, and stout bristles) had been accidentally left on the hood of my car, I assumed it was gone for good. Most likely I had been distracted by the need to unplug the umbilical cord that we Northerners use to connect the cars engine block heater to the mother power source, embedded in the parking lot barrier. Driving along, I pictured my handy device buried in a pile of snow, or flung into space and crushed by passing wheels in the street. To my surprise, three days later, my next scheduled workday, I spied my old helpmate, neatly placed on the metal divider directly in front of my usual nosing-in place—begging to be found. Thank you, who ever passed by that night, for taking the time . . .

Some months ago, having trodden, in the dark, through inches of newly fallen snow, I was once again in the process of brushing the white stuff from the mound which is my old Toyota, when a cheerful voice caught my ear. I turned to see a parka-encased, smiling young woman on the way to the bingo hall half a block away. Stopping, she asked, "Would you like some help with that?" The offer took me by surprise—filled my heart with good cheer. Though I turned down her help, the warmth of that spontaneous gesture stays with me still.

Another instance of a stranger's concern comes to mind. It happened one bitterly cold February evening a couple of years back. Bundled up in my heavy coat, wool hat, fleece-lined boots, and insulated gloves, and having looked the shop door, I padded down the back entrance hallway and noticed one of the street people lingering just outside the exit door, perhaps waiting for a friend. My coming through the door must have surprised him. I initially had a sense of vulnerability but decided to venture out and excuse myself as I walked around him. I was disarmed by his soft-voiced fatherly greeting "Take care now." His kind dark eyes and alcohol scented words, dispelled any notion of fear on my part and replaced it with concern. As I walked the two blocks to my car, in the biting chill, I thought of the man's bare hands and his less than adequate jacket. I warmed-up a sluggish engine, delivered the shop's deposits at the bank, and doubled back to see if my well-wisher was still there. I drove slowly, prepared to stop and offer him an extra pair of gloves that I keep in the car or a ride, if he needed one. He was nowhere to be seen . . .

*N*icknamed **Big Dog** because of his large stature and good-natured disposition, my brother, Jared Cook, had enjoyed the security of a nurturing family throughout his twenty-two years when he suddenly found himself confronted by a most severe test. He had been waterskiing with a group of friends on the day he was diagnosed with leukemia.

Despite every treatment available, the cancer aggressively ravaged Jared's body. When chemotherapy caused him to lose his hair, his father and brothers shaved their heads in a loving gesture of support. One night, while he endured doing a second round of chemotherapy, I stayed with him at the hospital, which gave us a quiet opportunity to talk.

I confided to Jared an experience I had had about two weeks before the cancer was identified. School, work, friends, and other relationships were all going well. My family was healthy, and I treasured the close association we enjoyed with one another. But the feeling that something terrible was going to happen didn't leave me. I didn't know what it might be, so I prayed every morning and every night for the welfare of my family.

Jared replied that he had experienced the same foreboding. Only his prayer had been, "If anything is going to happen, let it be me instead of someone I love."

Everyone's store of faith is different; my brother's circumstances did not reduce his. As the weeks went by, he lost sixty pounds, and his posture became stooped. Despite great pain and numerous other challenges, he kept a sense of humor and willingly submitted to whatever treatment

147

the doctors prescribed.

Death held no fear for Jared, yet he really wanted to live. He wanted to go to college and struggle, as he described. He wanted to marry and have children.

It was not to be.

Of life's making, not of his choosing, Jared accepted the inevitable with grace and humility. Even when confronted with a death sentence, he refused to let self-pity control his actions.

Near the end, it was a struggle for him to speak. Family members could barely hear his hoarsely whispered "I love you" as they entered the hospital room.

No matter how brief, every life leaves a legacy. With faith strong enough to withstand life's cross-examination, Jared R. Cook courageously passed his test on December 14. 1999.

I was born in the Highlands of Scotland in a little village on the Black Isle. My whole world was my home, my garden, and my brothers. I was the oldest and very sure of everything.

That all changed when I was five and went to school. Suddenly I knew nothing. My mother took me there and left me for the whole morning, and again in the afternoon. The other children were noisy, laughing and confident, and they had skills I could hardly begin. I was told that the headmaster, who carried a leather strap for discipline, knew that I had brains and would make a scholar out of me. I wanted to run away and never go back, but I did not dare to. I felt frightened, laughed at, and as if I must be very stupid.

It was my Aunty Nan, my father's sister, who rescued me. She was another Mackay, with wild, black hair as thick as mine. She knew how afraid I was, but she also knew how much I needed to be at school. She visited us on Sundays, and I can remember her week after week persevering with me. "Get your paper, Elizabeth," she said. "We will do the sums together. You'll enjoy them when you get the hang of it!" She always had time to help and never lost patience with me.

She was as determined as a mule, but her heart was the biggest I knew. I could not disappoint her; she would not allow me to. And eventually I settled down, and to my amazement discovered that I actually enjoyed arithmetic, grammar, reading and spelling.

At age ten I finally graduated to the master's room, with awe and trembling. How could I possibly match up? Surprise

149

again, I loved arithmetic sessions and English grammar. Even learning the Bible, parrot-fashion, held a joy. I loved to learn, and to please.

And there where discoveries of other talents, such as getting the Mercury out of Mr. Matheson's barometer by using a drinking straw, and blowing the little silver balls across our desks, that is until we were caught. I also discovered firsthand the use of his leather strap, when a few of us girls went for a walk during lunchtime to study the frogs and newts in a pond. Looking back I think he was actually frightened we had come to some harm.

It is sixty years since I started school in Munlochy. I still think of my Aunt with gratitude for the time she spent in teaching me. And of Mr. Matheson for caring so much that he poured his energy into teaching us unwilling, unruly or frightened children and showed us a love of learning, and to have the courage to try all things.

He had little hair and behind his back we called him 'Baldy', just as we called Aunt Nan 'Hairy Nanny'. Children can be cruelly honest! They both knew it, and forgave us. I hope they also knew how much they enriched our lives, mine in particular, with memories of happiness and a legacy of wealth in the mind.

Carlos Perez
Sales & Marketing Director

Having grown up in Bogotá, Columbia, I was always aware of the poverty that surrounded many in my native country. Nevertheless, as a child I was not known for being very giving. I guess this could be justified by saying that growing up with six sisters and two brothers you always have to share pretty much all you own—your clothes, toys, and of course the room. But if through the years I learned the real meaning of sharing, I have to give credit and thanks to the great example my mother was to me.

Back in her days the tradition was that children would be named after the Saint celebrated on the day you were born, and my mom happened to be born on October 2nd, the day of the Angels of Custody or Caring Angels, therefore the name given to her was Angelica Custodia or "Caring Angelica," and she surely has lived up to her name. Fond memories come to mind when I think of her.

Ever since I can remember, my mom would collect all the clothing that everybody in the family could no longer use, pack it in a suitcase and put it away on the top shelf of her closet. These items, along with others that her friends would give her, stayed there until she had the opportunity to go back to her hometown and offer them to those she knew were much in need.

I clearly remember as a child and later as a teenager being at her brother's house up in the northern part of Columbia, and having his living room full of visitors—most of them distant relatives, neighbors or friends who had heard that Custodia was once again in town. It was like a fashion show. People we did not even know would come in and out of my uncle's room trying

151

on the clothes that my mom had collected.

I remember the smiles and expressions of gratitude on the faces of many who for most of their lives had never had new clothes, and that by the time they would meet with my mother, would still be wearing the very same clothing she had given them during her last visit two years earlier.

These fond memories have left engraved on my heart a very clear message my mother taught me through her example: It does not matter how much you have, it is how much you are willing to give that brings real happiness to your life. All of us can be a Caring Angel to many who are not as privileged as we are.

When asked what inspired me to be the best at what I do, I have to say it was my father. As a young boy, I would hand tools to him as he shoed horses. By the time I was eleven I was trimming the horses' feet. When I was fourteen I was doing everything. I was never allowed to go to a friend's house to have fun. After my father finished his job working for the county (and I was at school), he would schedule horses to be shod in the evening. We had a reputation that we could and would shoe any horses; therefore we took care of a lot of horses that were easily frightened, bad mannered and very dangerous. When I graduated from high school, I started a farrier business of my own. From this experience I learned how to work hard and how to move around a horse.

While working for my father, it seemed I never quite measured up. He said a lot of things that would have broken most people's self-esteem. After hearing how I would never amount to anything and how stupid I was, I became even more determined to prove him wrong.

When asked what made me excel I would have to say that when I started forging in a hot fire at age nineteen, I knew I could do better after every completed shoe. Not SHOULD do better, but COULD. It's only a few letters difference, but it completely changes your outlook and attitude. I started going to an old blacksmith in Idaho about eight hours for my home. He was from the old school, kind of like my father, so he didn't scare me off. He taught me most of what I know about forging.

153

One way a farrier/ blacksmith or in common terms, horseshoer gains education is by competing in contests that are usually accompanied by a clinic from a respected and renowned farrier. I started to compete in 1983. The contestants are given a piece of bar stock and are told to make a certain shoe. There are many kinds of shoes from all over the world. Most come from Europe. A certain amount of time is allotted and then all shoes are judged. In a contest it's not just one or two pairs of shoes that win, several rounds are completed lasting two or three days.

Contests are held all over the world, the most take place in America, England, Scotland or Canada.

Everyone looks forward to and talks about the one held during the Calgary stampede in Alberta, Canada in July. It is the world Champion blacksmith competition. In 1984, I won the title of world Champion blacksmith. I was the only American to win this title until 1999. I am still the youngest participant to win it age 23. In the year 2000, I was voted one of the top 25 most Influential Farriers in the industry and in 2003 I was inducted into the International Horseshoeing Hall of Fame.

I have been to England, Scotland, France, Japan, Québec, Alberta, Alaska and every state in the lower 48 teaching clinics and judging contests.

I guess I proved my father wrong. No one decides who you are except yourself.

The two greatest gifts in my life are my children, Derek who is seventeen and Brad who is fifteen. They have taught me to never give up. I never knew, and nobody could come close to telling me about this beautiful love I feel for them. I never thought I could love anyone or anything as much as I love my boys.

Through the years they have given me the gifts of patience, love, joy, sorrow, pain and unconditional love. Some of these things have hurt, some have not, but I realize that I need to experience all of these emotions in order for me to progress and succeed in life. They make me want to be a better person, mom, wife and friend. And no matter what is said or done, they without doubt help carry me through life. I have done many stupid things in this lifetime.

After a bitter divorce, my ex-husband's retained custody of the children for about one year. Let me just say that it nearly killed me. Looking back on things I now realize that I was so worried about how it would affect the way they felt about me. Would they hate me or blame me for things that were not in my control. I never imagined that they would continue to simply love me through that year. It should have been me, but they are the ones that picked me up, brushed me off and said "Let's start again, mom." I got custody a year later.

It is not a matter of if I will fall, but when I will fall, and it truly is how you rise from your fall that makes a difference. I felt like a let my kids down and I had a hard time forgiving myself. The boys forgave me, then I just had to forgive

155

myself, until I realized "Why shouldn't I forgive myself."

All in all they are my pillars of strength and Derek, I love you so much and I am so proud of you. You are handsome and soft of heart and I love telling people that you are my son. Brad, you are the kindest, sweetest boy a mother could have. I love you so much just the way you are, you touch my heart every day. I am sorry for the rough few years, but I am so looking forward to the future.

From the bottom of my heart,
Mom

S. Floyd Mori

National President,
Japanese American Citizens League (JACL)
International Business Consultant

I can still clearly remember the times when neighborhood children showered racial slurs on me whenever I may have gotten the best of them at some of the games children play. I was always cast as the "Indian" rather than the "cowboy" or the "robber" rather than the righteous "cop." Often it was literally unpleasant to be who I was.

These experiences helped me to develop a resentment of who I was as a Japanese American born of immigrant parents from Japan. I often wondered to myself, why I was born Japanese rather than white like the rest of the kids. While the other children proudly invited their parents to school events and to parent-teacher conferences, I was ashamed to invite my parents as they spoke little English and did not act the same as the parents of the other children. It was a time when it was not cool to look like the enemy let alone speak a language that was often belittled in the movies and radio. I was humiliated in the first grade when I was the only one not invited to the birthday party of a classmate.

As I matured, I developed an attitude that I had to perform better than the other kids in order to mitigate the reality of being different. Thus, in school I studied harder and played at sports harder than most in order to win some praise and acceptance. My abilities grew and I began to excel in academic subjects and in sports. With this came the acceptance that I hungered for and needed in an achievement-oriented society.

157

I did not understand at the time that it was who I was and what my parents were that were the main ingredients to my positive development as a human being. The cultural values that my parents instilled in me as a child are the key factors that enabled me to progress. It was not the values of my classmates or the ethics of their parents. It was some of the deep cultural values that were taught to me by example at home rather than in the classroom. Much later I came to realize the hardships my parents endured to make a better life for their family.

Maturity helped to bring a better understanding of who I was and what my parents were. The hard work ethic that I endured as a boy and young man raised on a vegetable tuck farm was basic to all that I did throughout my school life. I remember the praise of my coach when I was in junior high school when he elevated me as an example of physical fitness that other athletes should emulate. It was none of my doing, but the result of a Father who understood that his young son should do his share of the farm work during the summer time.

"Gambate! Gambate!" This was my Father telling me to bear the suffering and hardship. It was the equivalent of today's admonishment to "hang in there." When confronted with any little hardship, it is very easy to give up or take on something easier. Hanging in there earned me an advanced college degree and a desirable job teaching college economics. It won me a political election in which nobody gave me a chance, and it helped me to work with my wife to raise five children of whom anybody would be proud.

Being loyal to family and friends was basic to what my parents exemplified in their dealings with their fellow man. They were loyal to the United States even in light of the fact that the law at that time did not allow them to become citizens. They had no hesitation in sending two of their sons off to War as soldiers in the United States Army to help protect the freedoms and privileges they enjoyed as immigrants. Their oldest son returned in a casket, yet it was a proud day many years later when both of my parents were given the right of citizenship in this great country.

The pride that I enjoy today with family, friends, and country is what I learned from understanding who I was and what my parents were. So today I express my gratitude to my great Father and Mother, who helped me to finally understand that who I am is the most valuable asset I have. For any material gain, the praise of my fellow men, the joy of watching my family grow, and the enjoyment I receive by living in this great country, I am indebted to my parents. While ignorance fostered a feeling of shame in me as a Japanese American child, understanding has developed a great sense of gratitude for my parents and for all they did for me.

Anca Student
University Student

I close my eyes; think about people, things, facts, words, situations that changed something in me. I think about my parents—my mother. Only last month I realized that I stayed nine months in the dark, inside of her. I wonder if it seemed a long time for me then, or if I would have wanted to be somewhere else— No. It was a step, a period in my life and everything was developing in an internal, natural rhythm. NOW where is the rhythm —everything is running around with closed eyes.

I'm looking at my mother; —she's working eight hours a day in a factory, doing the same thing, a monotone thing, in the same rhythm, working with her hands, breathing in toxic air, surrounded by noisy machines. She seems so naive, so pure, so blind. She's alone and I'm alone—but I know that I am alone.

She doesn't have friends, I think she has her colleagues, we all have colleagues. She has a family which is pretty fond of her; she has her religion and maybe it is not as routine a religion as I consider it to be. She's beautiful if you know what beautiful means. That doesn't mean that I don't fight or disagree with her almost all the time, or that she speaks the same language as I, but it doesn't mean either that my language is the correct one.

For sure she made the first change in me, bringing me into this experience called life, human life. It was not my intention to write about my mother and her emptiness or foolishness. I don't want to write about anyone or anything in particular considering that only a trauma can change you suddenly and all the other changes are a total of the surrounding people, actions and facts. You wake up in a morning or I woke up in the morning, after reading Dostoyevsky, or Pappini, or Antonio Lobo Antunes; after you read there about yourself, after you read yourself in people that walk on the streets of New York or Scrind, the small village where my grandparents are living, and after you see your mother, see the noisy fight between your neighbors, or the silence of a street child, or you hear the friend of the fruit seller telling you with a smile to enjoy your banana, or maybe see tones of common and uncommon movies, or just meet your friend, or just leave your friend. You wake up that morning, look in the mirror, feel the blood and bones inside of you and ask: Who am I? A long question and when it appears—I won't write further because here are only words. I'll see life and maybe find an answer or forget the question.

161

Elaine Wolf
Student of Life

My parents were my first mentors. My mother always read to me, she loved books. She told me when I was a baby in a high chair I wouldn't eat unless a book was propped in front of me. Soon, I was watching and correcting her, when from utter boredom, she skipped words. Anyway, by three years old I was reading newspapers to my beloved father, who died from cancer when he was sixty-five.

We were very poor, but I didn't know that and we had excellent council housing, one downstairs room was the width of the house and was covered in polished cupboards, the top one full of books!

So my next mentors were these books, or rather their authors—Dickens, Hardy, Shakespeare (complete works), the Bible, Darwin's Theory, Marx, Tolstoy, Austen, Brontes, Dostoyevsky, Kipling, Alexander Dumas, a lot of poetry and others—Marie Corelli's books, "Zola", "Rise and Fall of the Roman Empire", "Wealth of Nations" and a great deal of mid-Victorian rubbish about good little girls who died and went to heaven and bad little girls who went to hell! "The History of the British People in pictures" which gave me a love and interest in history I have to this day. I still have the original book, every page loose from so much reading. When I was about ten, my mother's friend lent me Arthur Mee's Children's Encyclopedia, ten volumes and in my methodical way I read from volume one in order, (never mind the different subjects.)

I was born in Pontllanfraith, Monmothshire, Wales. The place had no library. However, I read the whole of the school library twice.

I obtained a scholarship for Pontllanfraith Grammar School with another library to peruse including lots of biographies and travel books, also books on Chinese religions and John Donne and French books etc.

Here, I met another mentor, the history teacher Ms. Phillips. She nurtured my love for history. I obtained my matriculation certificates with four distinctions, one of which was in history. Ms. Phillips told me what she should not have, but that mark was the highest in Wales that year and a record for the school. There was one slight difficulty, I was just sixteen and although I was given a seat at Cardiff University I had to wait until I was eighteen to take my seat. "Is there any difficulty about money?" my dear Ms. Phillips asked, and standing there with my broken glasses, with the soles of my shoes parting company with the uppers, I replied, "No, Miss," with the stubborn proudness of the very poor.

She told me that she had been asked if she could supply Boots the Chemist with a girl to help out in the shop. She gave me the right to go to the school for books and then go to her house anytime to use her wonderful library and she said she would continue tutoring me. She was a wonderful teacher. I never forget anything she told me in any lesson.

I started work as a shop assistant in Boots, and a man from the head office told me that with my qualifications(distinction in Biology) they would send me to Nottingham University on a full salary, I only had to sign an agreement to work for them a certain number of years. I said I would think about it. Meanwhile I started studying forensic pharmacy, dispensing, Latin, pharmacognosy and physiology—but history was my love. But for that I would have to persuade my father to take a private

163

grant of money and he loathed charity, or anything resembling it.

Still, it never happened, any of it, because something very dark happened to me one night on my way home from a dance. My life ended there, that is, the life I thought would be mine. I never told anyone.

Some years went by and a public library opened in Blackwood—what a ray of sunshine. Freud, Milton, and the librarian could get me any book I wanted— Plato's Republic, the Iliad and the Odyssey.

Then I met a Hungarian, my second husband, Imre D. Wolf, whose family had a 700 year history of being master bakers and confectioners as was he. Imre completely changed my life; I couldn't understand why he, who was so devastatingly handsome, could love me. After several accidents in the pit, he left and opened his own bakery and shops in Pontyprod and he had this house built for me, my children (eventually five) and later in life, my mother. At that time, I had low self-esteem, was very self-conscious and introverted, damaged goods, cowardly, of no worth at all.

He changed all that—first he made me take driving lessons—was I ever nervous. I wanted to work so I got a job in an Italian restaurant as a waitress, then against my will he made me apply for a job as a GPO telephonist, which to my surprise, they gave me. Slowly my self-esteem rose. And there were other jobs and travel abroad, all at my husband's insistence. I am grateful to him for giving me the gift of self-worth once more. My life has been much richer because of his influence and belief in me.

I have pondered the question of who has been the greatest influence in my life, and outside of my family, I've come up with the general group called teachers. I haven't had a close relationship with the few I consider the biggest influences, but because of what I learned from them, they have directed some of the choices I have made during my lifetime.

My second piano teacher, Irving Wassermann, was one who required me to learn the techniques of music. He was born in Poland, studied in Vienna and Brussels, and lived in New York for a short period of time. He was struggling financially, hardly making ends meet. Then he heard he could earn $10 by playing a piece on the radio. He got the opportunity to do so, and a conductor of an orchestra heard him play and offered him a position with the symphony. He practiced diligently, but three days before his performance, his hands and fingers were swollen to the point that he was unable to play. When he went to the doctor he found out that he had arthritis and needed to be in a dry climate. He had a friend attending Utah State University in Logan, a small town in northern Utah, so he thought he would spend a few weeks with him to see how his hands would respond to a different location. He fell in love with Logan and has been there sixty years teaching children and adults the skills and love of classical music.

As an adolescent, I really did not appreciate what he required of me. It seems so simple, but counting was an important skill I was lacking at the time I started with him. It was a struggle for me at

165

first because when the previous teacher played the piece through for me, I could remember how to play it. Mr. Wassermann required me to count out loud and thus my weakness was apparent. Since then I have accompanied a variety of people in singing, in playing instruments and in playing duets. All of this requires precise timing. I would have been unable to do so without his persistence in teaching me what I needed to know. Because of what I learned from him, I have had wonderful experiences in sharing music with others. Because I played classical music, I gained an appreciation for the beauty, the emotional experience, and the peace it can bring.

He said that learning music is like learning all kinds of math. You learn to appreciate, participate, and enjoy without having to be a math or musical genius. I'm far from being the musical genius, but because of my association with my piano teacher and the skills he taught me, my life has been musically enriched. Not everyone has the opportunity to come in contact with someone who loves what he does like Irving Wasserman. I am blessed.

If anyone had asked me what my impression of a Renaissance person was several years ago, I would have offered some stuttered reply about a strapping young Italian painter or scholar. Today, however, a far different picture rests in my mind. In place of the dark, romantic Italian, I see an old man, Irish cap resting upon his bald head as he sits behind the wheel of his yellow convertible. The qualities of humanism and intellect that I once saw only in the great works of Michelangelo shine brighter in the form of my grandfather, Jack Alex McDonald.

The greats of the Renaissance were men with talent and interest in many areas —sculpture, architecture, science, poetry, painting, and engineering. My grandfather was such a man, his interests spanning from geology to card games. He taught school for the fifth, sixth, and seventh grades for many years before advancing to a job in community development at the University of Utah. His education and knowledge was remarkably well rounded. He directed a summer science program for elementary school students yet "knew the answer to any possible question about literature," says my father. Grandpa was a skilled writer, creating movie scripts for the University, and compiling his personal history as well as many of his ancestors. He loved math and music, helped establish a McDonald family legacy of singers, pianists and instrumentalists. He had a remarkable vocabulary, and my father claims it was impossible to beat him at any type of word game. Grandpa also had an extraordinary love and gift for languages. While in Brazil for a few years he learned to speak

167

Portuguese with a fluency and beauty that he kept the remaining years of his life.

Grandpa not only enjoyed intellectual pursuits, but athletics as well. He loved fishing, camping, and shooting, but like his own father, his greatest love was baseball. I remember Grandpa taking my sisters and me on a ride in his yellow convertible with the oh-so-hot black leather seats, and having him tell us stories of his father taking him to ballgames and how they would splurge and spend $5 on hot dogs and snacks. Now, as I listen to my father tell about the games Grandpa took him to, I can't help but smile every time I sit in the Kingdome eating peanuts with my dad.

Grandpa loved photography, traveling, auto mechanics and history—the list could go on and on. Most importantly, Grandpa loved his family and his God. Like the true Renaissance man, Grandpa was more than a well-rounded intellectual- he led a balanced spiritual life. There was never any question about his commitments to his faith. He held family prayer and taught his children by example.

As I listened to my father talk about the great brain of his father, I confess I felt some amazement. This intellectual giant was not the man I thought I knew. The man I remember was so warm, so personable, so endearing, that the light of his character far outshone his incredible intellect. I remember sitting captivated, listening to stories, or laughing with delight at his dry wit. Grandfather was the father of eight children, had well over thirty grandchildren and six great-grandchildren—but there were no bounds to his love. I remember looking around during his funeral at my aunts, uncles, and cousins and seeing how much they were crying. I realized then that my grandfather had a special gift, because he made everyone feel that he or she was his personal favorite. My grandfather was a true humanist, for he knew the worth of the human soul.

Perhaps the achievements of my grandfather don't seem so marvelous to the outside eye. He wasn't famous or rich and his closest friends existed chiefly within his family. I, however, see it much differently. I see my grandfather's achievements as the greatest any human soul can hope for—the peace and happiness of his children.

I see my grandfather whenever my dad cracks a joke, when I watch my brothers play baseball, when I think of my sister's gift for languages, and whenever I look down with some dismay at my white Irish skin. The great masters of the Renaissance left their mark on the world, indelibly printed on the forefront of history with works like the Mona Lisa or David. My grandfather's mark is one that will not grow dusty with age or fade with the passing of years, for it is breathing and will be shining for generations to come.

169

Suzanne Labrum
Clown

I don't remember all of their names but I'll always remember how they made me feel. I'm a professional clown and I mostly perform at birthday parties.

Recently, a mother called me to book a party. Her husband and seven-year-old son had been in a terrible snowmobile accident. The boy was taken to the Primary Children's Medical Center and that's where they had the party, in a room large enough to fit all his siblings, grandparents, etc. And then they wheeled the little boy in on his hospital bed. Well, I did my silly warm-up stuff and then launched into my comedy magic show. I needed to stay close to his bed because he had to lay flat but I had to entertain everyone else also. (It was quite a challenge).

He paid full attention to me and I made him smile a couple of times and at my funny, grand finale, he laughed. As the nurses wheeled him back to his room, one of them told me that was the first time he had smiled in three weeks! I was glad to bring some happiness to that child and walked on clouds back to my car.

Sometimes I do parties where a small child is either very shy or is really afraid of clowns. If the parents will stay in the room and sit with their child in the back, I can have them slowly inch forward until he's sitting with the rest of the kids. By the end of the magic show, they are hugging me and holding on to me. And they will allow me to paint their faces! I get so much satisfaction in bringing a child to participate with the other kids, and especially to stop being afraid. They can see that I'm "safe."

I always leave every party with everyone having fun and being happier than when I first walked in the door. It's a good feeling. When it's time to leave the children almost always swarm around me, begging me not to go and telling me that they love me. I have never left a party with people unhappy.

Whatever these people get from my performance I receive so much satisfaction, feel appreciated and my self-esteem takes another leap forward.

Every one of the many people I have encountered over the last fourteen years that I've been a clown has touched my heart and left a warm spot there. They have made me a better person when I'm out of makeup. I will always and forever remember those children (some stand out more than others) and the gift of true acceptance they have given to me to feel and treasure!

Jerry Pam
Publicist

*I*t is extremely difficult to state the one event that changes one's life. As far as I'm concerned it could be one of any number and the reader might have a different interpretation of each situation.

For example could it be my decision to emigrate to Australia with my parents as I was never achieving any success in my native England. After three years another, what seemed like a momentous decision, was my desire to come to Hollywood and seek my fame and fortune. After having been offered a job at 20th Century Fox and securing a wife, I arrived in Los Angeles only to discover there was no position at the studio.

However I was determined to make good in fantasy land and through a lucky chance of fate I had the opportunity to graduate from being a journalist to repre-senting motion pictures and personalities as a publicist. A producer friend, who had changed his profession from being a publi-cist, called me from his London mansion and really changed my life by hiring me to represent film that was destined to star a musical group that would to become the outstanding recording artists of the 20th century.

Thus my life changed with represen-tation of the movie career of The Beatles and through their two motion pictures "A Hard Day's Night" and "Help!"

Little did I know that my phone would ring more times in one day then in a month with journalists, fans, celebrities all wanting to meet the Fab 4. I really discov-ered that it's who you know rather than what you know that enables one to become successful in the very dog eat dog profession of show business.

This one situation really changed my life as I was able to secure clients for my publicity office purely because of my association with these giants. Maybe this was the turning point because for the past 40 years which is more than half of my life I have enjoyed the fruits of success.

173

Elizabeth Foxwell
Mystery Writer / Editor

I count the spring of 1983 as one of the most memorable periods of my life, in which I studied in London on the University of Maryland study abroad program.

Hampered by ligaments torn in my foot practically on arrival in England, I nonetheless was embraced by a Boulogne hat store proprietor because of my rusty French; was told by a Canterbury china store clerk (and American enthusiast) that he wanted to be buried in Brooklyn; constantly forgot to use the work "queue" instead of "line," prompting puzzled looks; and was rescued by two kindly bus station workers when I misjudged the time of the next bus from Stratford-upon-Avon.

Most of all, I learned the value of multiple perspectives and the richness of British and Irish history, which also presented a conflict in my emphatically English surname and strong maternal Irish background.

I stood in the small pink house where my Irish grandfather had been born, met one of his childhood friends, and saw the trunk in which my great-uncle, who had survived a bullet in his brain during the Anglo-Irish war, stored his ammunition as a member of an IRA "Flying Column." When I walked into my cousin's remote, peat-warmed cottage, greeting me was my parents' wedding photograph on the wall.

The experience had long lasting effects: I worked in international education for six years; my younger brother was inspired by my example to study in Vienna and Geneva, leading to his career in international human resources; and, working from information from my Irish relatives,

174

I reunited my mother with a long-lost cousin, who had been separated from the family after his parents' premature deaths. It was a quest for not only historical but also cross-cultural and personal understanding that has greatly affected my life. And the foot still bothers me from time to time.

Angela Pawsey
Rose Specialist

It is simple to say that the most influential person in your life is one of your parents. For me this is true. My Grandmother a Cant had two daughters. The youngest, Diana, married my Father. My Grandmother continued to run the family firm of Benjamin R. Cant and Sons founded in 1765 after her husband's death. However, her oldest daughter Joan was a musician and Diana, whilst having an interest in the firm soon had children to look after.

My father fortunately had never loved his work with a seed merchant and was delighted to leave his desk job and starting from the bottom he learned the business of growing, showing and selling roses. He came from a farming family and was therefore ideally suited as we also grew arable crops side by side with roses. Many Rose growers do not have the luxury of the farmland needed to provide the ideal rotation of crops to produce top-quality roses.

Unfortunately my mother fell ill when I was very young and died when I was ten years old. My eldest brother Martin, who took on the farming mantle at age eighteen, believes I never saw my mother when she was healthy, and this may well be the reason why my father was so important in my life as he had to contend with three young children, an ailing wife, and a very hard job.

You could say that Martin, and my other Brother Roger knew little but farming and Rose Growing in our early years. It was natural for Roger to follow in my Father's footsteps. At the young age of four he took his first steps to "Showing" flowers.

He cut off the heads of all the Tulips in the garden and threaded them through a garden seat. Having received his initial training with Dicksons of Newtownard in Northern Ireland Roger took over the Growing of the roses, while my Dad reluctantly took a more office oriented position.

I did not mind going into the business. I had during holiday times been involved with some aspects of the firm, and helped Dad on my school days getting the paperwork ready for a "round." A term used to calculate which plants were needed to be lifted for the orders being dispatched the next day. It was a job which took up most of dad's evenings in November and December of each year.

Probably due to my mother's illness I had always wanted to be a nurse, and at eighteen this is what I started to do. However I was a very shy, nervous person and strangely I do not feel I was tough enough to be a nurse. Having left after only a few months I had no real idea of what else to do. Dad said I could come into the business provided I learned typing and shorthand at night classes. So again my father influenced my future and the firm remains.

If my father had not married my mother who knows if Cants of Colchester LTD as our firm is now known would be around for over three hundred thirty years.

When I was twenty-one the then Rose Distribution Association was looking for a Secretary, and my father suggested I could do it. I became Secretary of that and then later of a combined association called British Rose Growers Association. This led me to produce an annual booklet for the Rose industry called "Find that Rose" which listed nearly all the roses in commerce in the UK and the members growing them.

My father had a very hard life what with losing my mother very early in their marriage, seeing my stepmother suffer from mini-strokes, and later himself suffering with Parkinson's disease, but he loved his life with roses. His wish was to die as he put it "with his boots on." He didn't quite get his wish, but worked into his 80s and died years later in 1997. My brothers and I are rushing toward our own official retirement ages, so who knows what the future holds. The younger generation would like to see the firm continue but also have their own individual jobs and interests outside the firm. What one can be sure of is that my Father guaranteed that the name of Cants in rose growing continues.

MARY

Carol Thiel
Flight Attendant

My life has been inspired and influenced by many people and places but the single most influential person was my younger sister Mary.

She spent only thirty-six short years with us, but in that time taught more people about life and the curveballs it can throw that anyone I know.

She came into this world with the challenge of spina bifida at a time when not much hope was available. She beat all the odds and survived. Not only survived but flourished and blossomed into a beautiful young woman. People flocked to her because of her strong soul and positive outlook on life.

She endured many painful operations, always with the hope that this would improve her life and it did. She owned her own home, drove her own car, bowled and even walked five miles for March of Dimes to raise money for those less fortunate.

When she died at the age of thirty-six of cancer people from all walks of life came to her memorial service to tell stories of how her courage and love of life helped them turn their own lives around to become productive and inspired people.

So when I am having a hard time dealing with life's challenges I give a glance skyward to see and hear Mary's beautiful soul.

179

William C. Wall
Concierge

I was born into a military family in September of 1972. For me the military was no choice, it was family tradition. After all my great-grandfather died in World War I, my grandfather died in World War II, my natural father served four tours of duty in Vietnam, my stepfather did a tour in Vietnam, and my mother was a drill instructor in the Air Force. I joined the military two weeks after high school graduation, passing up a scholarship to a four-year acting school.

I spent three and a half years in the Army and served in combat in both Desert Storm and Somalia. I was medically discharged from service for hearing loss and Post-Traumatic Stress Disorder (PTSD). A friend I had served with in combat was born and raised in Fairbanks, Alaska, and wanted me to come up and meet his family. This being back in April of 1996 and I have yet to really leave.

While here in Fairbanks I started going to Mr. Swan, a VA counselor to try and help me with some of the nightmares and other things that my combat experience dredges up now and again. The darkest times are when you're alone, when you think of the soldiers who didn't make it back. Sometimes people tell me that it was difficult to watch the treatment of American soldiers in Somalia on television.

My answer is, "You should have been there. The movie 'Black Hawk Down' portrayed my unit."

Mr. John Swan has helped me out quite a bit. He calls things the way he sees them and since he has gone through the same experiences as I, only earlier, he has the knowledge and experience to deal with situations like mine. I'm now enrolled at the local university to get my bachelors degree in computer science.

If it were not for my coming up to Alaska and getting in touch with Mr. Swan I would be doing time in a mental institution or what I consider to be wasting space on this earth for not being able to cope or deal with certain situations that arise.

I like it here in Alaska, there are lots of things to do and the people are friendly and helpful, even though sometimes the local mosquitoes look big enough to carry off your first-born.

Pat Soutar
Foster Parent

As well as raising our own children, my husband and I looked after many foster children. One who made the greatest impression upon us was a timid little girl called Mary. She was just five years of age when she came into our care with her two sisters aged three, and eighteen months.

Always shy and retiring it was clear from the start that Mary was the mother of the two younger ones and fiercely protective of them if she thought they might be hurt or troubled in any way. She had so much love to give, and as we gave to her, we received a great measure in return.

As the weeks went by and she learned to trust us, she became a little girl again, learning to laugh and play. Gradually, as she knew her sisters were safe, the weight of the world fell from her little frame. For a brief time she could think of herself.

We were very sad when she went home to her mother, especially as she was reluctant to go, but I'll never forget her courage, when she was scarcely more than a baby herself, and her care for those even younger.

As a secondary school girl I had a P.E. teacher called Mrs. Wilson. I looked up to admire this lovely kind lady greatly. Although I was hopeless at P.E. being small and plump, and I hated games, she never made me feel inadequate or embarrassed, always encouraging me to do my best and take part. I rarely heard her shout at any pupil or become impatient with us, although we were a pretty motley crew! Her wrath was reserved for girls who were behaving very badly or dangerously.

Mrs. Wilson taught First Aid Classes for adults and children for the British Red Cross one evening a week, and managed to coax me through my first aid exam several times despite my nervousness and self-consciousness. She created in me a love for the work, and a belief that I could succeed. She encouraged me in my desire to make it my career, and when I left school and went to Stornoway in the Outer Hebrides to begin my nursing training.

On one of my periods of leave I was greatly saddened to learn that Mrs. Wilson had died. She would only have been in her fifties. Unknown to her pupils she had been ill for sometime, but unselfishly had hidden it from us. Nearly twenty years later I can still see her smiling gently in my mind's eye, encouraging me, and making me believe that if I did my best I would succeed, and I still think of her fondly, now that I do what I love: psychiatric nursing.

183

Trisha Fitzgerald Carter
Domestic Engineer

Being the youngest of four children, I was so excited when my mom became pregnant! I vowed that I would get up half an hour earlier every morning to brush the baby's hair. I was going to take her everywhere with me. I wouldn't be like some big sisters who thought their younger siblings were just tag 'alongs'. I wouldn't be alone anymore. I was only seven.

Everyone thought the baby was going to be a boy. A name had even been chosen—Mark Benjamin. I was the only one who knew it would be a girl.

But tragedy struck. I remember the night I got the news, October 9th, 1975. My mom was on her bed. She called me in and told me the baby had died. They didn't know why, she just quit growing. I cried and cried and cried. I am sure my mom thought I was just being a drama queen.

I'm not sure why I took it so hard. I have always felt alone, that I was on my own with no one to confine in. A little sister was an answer to my loneliness. We would do everything together and we would be best friends.

The baby was considered full-term and was born about four weeks later on November 2nd, 1975. She was small, only three pounds, but perfectly formed with dark hair. I never got to see her, but my mom told me.

Over the next several years, every birthday wish, every wishing pond we passed, whether it be a restaurant or Disneyland, I wished that Trudy, for that is what my dad had named her, would come back to me. I cried and mourned over this little sister so many times I cannot put a number on it. I

184

prayed and prayed for her to come back to me.

When I turned twelve things got a little easier. I guess I started to grow up. But I still thought about how much love I would have had for my little sister.

As the years went by, things happened. My dad died when I was fourteen. It was a shock. He died slow enough to see him turn into skin and bones as the cancer spread throughout his body. He lost fifteen pounds in one week. But it was quick enough for us not to realize it was happening.

When I was sixteen, I started to date a quiet guy. He was a senior and I was a sophomore. He was popular and I obviously had little self worth because I felt that I was only of value if I had a cool boyfriend. He wasn't very kind, but when you have self-defeating behaviors, you stay in relationships that may not be healthy. When I was seventeen, I became pregnant.

My mom, being wise, told me she would not let me marry this boy unless I could prove to her that I truly loved them. This was what I needed to hear. Within five weeks, I broke up with him and not only would I not marry him, I did not want him in my life at all. That was it. I walked away, we never resumed our relationship.

My family was very supportive and my pregnancy went very well. My religious leader tried to convince me to put my baby up for adoption so that it would have a father and mother. But I knew that I would always think about the baby. The uncertainty of its well-being would be such a torment for me to have to live with. I knew I needed to step up to the plate.

185

My mom had convinced me that my baby was a boy, which was smart. On October 9th, 1985, I went into labor. Mom threatened me not to have my baby on this date. Being so young the labor was slow. My mom took me to the hospital. My sister was my coach.

The whole time I was in labor I was so worried about what to name this boy. All I could come up with was Jake R.! R. what? I needed a middle name that started with an R. so I would have a J. R. Fitzgerald. Finally, the time came for me to push. Boy, if I would have seen those birthing films earlier, I would have never, ever had sex before or after marriage.

I cannot tell you how I felt, for words cannot describe the feelings in my heart when the doctor held up my baby and I saw that she was a little girl.

I think it was then that my mom realized how truly devastated I had been over the loss of her baby. When I saw my own little girl with her dark hair, I turned to my mom and said, "I've waited ten years for this, Mom." She replied, "I know, honey."

My Trudy turned eighteen a few months back. At her age, I had a four-month-old baby. I finished high school with my class, returning to school when she was three weeks old. Although I never had anything above a 3.5 GPA before the pregnancy, afterwards I was on the honor roll every quarter usually getting a 3.9 or 4.0. I went to college and did really well, making the Dean's List quite often.

My mom made sure I knew she had already raised her children and she would not raise mine. But I never wanted her to.

Over the years, Trudy has been my

186

very best friend. I married a wonderful man when she was six. It took a while for me to find the right one to be her daddy. I wasn't in a hurry. He adopted her three years later. I never put her biological father's name on the birth certificate. I did not feel he was worthy to have rights to this little bit of heaven. (By the way, I broke his heart, guess he should have been be nicer when he had a chance.)

With Trudy my weaknesses became my strengths because I knew it was my responsibility to teach her the right way. In the process I learned great lessons myself. Trudy has exceeded my expectations as a daughter and as a person. She's everything I had ever hoped for and as close to heaven as a person can be. My prayers were answered, Trudy came back to me and I'm not alone.

187

Irma Rapaport
PhD

The gaggle of nine-year-olds sat in a tight circle, talking and giggling while Ms. Rosa observed the interaction from the teacher's lounge. She watched the chubby and awkward little girl who sat in the fringes of the group, patiently waiting for a morsel of attention. She recognized the little girl's attempts to hide her loneliness behind a fixed smile. Ms. Rosa saw hope arise and die in the little girl's eyes when the occasional kindness was followed by further isolation. Recess ended and the girls trooped back to the classroom, laughing and talking, the lonely one trailing behind, unseen.

Poetry recitation followed recess and Ms. Rosa called the chubby little girl to the front of the class. The beauty of the poem was brought forth by her inner glow and intense feelings, expressed in the inflections of her voice and the graceful movement of her hands; her classmates snickered seeing only her chubbiness and awkwardness. Who had noticed how beautiful and expressive the little girl's hands were as she recited, Ms. Rosa softly asked in the silence that followed. A glowing smile transformed the little girl's face.

School ended and Ms. Rosa and watched the children gather for the walk home. They seemed to have felt the transformation that had occurred in the classroom and they were now able to see the little girl's radiance, her chubbiness forgotten. The circle opened and enveloped her. And as she walked away in the center of the group, the chubby little girl seemed to blossom, shielded by Ms. Rosa's words and her new sense of self.

Years have gone by and I have led a full and rewarding life, with more happiness and successes than pain or failures. Ms. Rosa's face is lost in the mists of time, but her words still guide my path and echo in my heart.

I have had many wonderful people who have been "sentinels" along life's path. Each one has been passionately involved in good causes, which have shaped and directed my life. Each one has had an amazing ability to love wisely. Beloved friendship has been the result.

Of late I have been drawn into the crusade to protect the innocence of children. As has always been my experience, involvement with a good cause has also brought with it the blessing of association with wonderful people. This involvement was to be no exception.

I was asked to speak at a convention in San Juan, and as I pondered my preparation for that opportunity, I could not stop thinking about a woman I had heard speak a few times and whose thoughts had greatly enlarged my own.

Whenever I had been in Tami Stillion's presence, I was reminded of Anne Morrow Lindbergh's book, Gift from the sea, when she says, "My life cannot implement in action all the demands of all the people to whom my heart responds." I felt drawn to Tami, but could never quite find the time to connect. I determined to simply ask. I telephoned and (not really fully appreciating the commitment I was seeking from a full-time mom of two young children, and a full-time student, at one of the nation's top photography schools) I asked Tami if she would put together a media presentation featuring her photos of children. She didn't even hesitate.

We had less than two weeks to complete the presentations and she had to juggle classes, photo shoots, and family commitments around almost constant rain

189

to catch the light necessary to artfully capture the heart of a child needing protection from abuse. It was a miracle! She did it! I didn't expect that she would be able to take time from school and family to travel with me to the convention, to make the presentation, but she did. We finally had the chance to come to know one another.

We had a week at the convention and saw incredible reactions to Tami's photo essay called "The Prayer of the Children." Hearts did respond and people mobilized into the fight for families. It was Tami's heart however that really touched mine, as she laughed and cried with me, staying up night after night to share life's experiences and enrich me with her insights. I am so grateful to have Tami's friendship. I count on her as another precious sentinel along life's path for me—a gift from God! Not only will her presence bolster me in my work, but also she has become a sentinel to children everywhere, as she offers through her photography, a triumph over pornography, and a message of hope to all.

Dear Mom,

It's been too long since I last wrote you and I have missed you so much. These days so many memories of my childhood flood back into my mind and for some reason all I can remember is how wonderful it was . . . like living in a "Father knows best," sitcom. When my life gets too hectic or complicated I like to step back and breathe for a moment and think about all that you were and all that you gave me.

You lived a small life. Raised in a loving home were money was scarce, you couldn't go to college even though you loved school and learning. Instead, you went to work at Woolworth's to help your parents and then married a boy you met at church. The two of you raised eight children together until cancer took your life when you were only fifty-eight. On the surface it may look like a small life but it was so much more.

I learned how to love by watching you. Somehow you convinced each one of us children that you loved us the best. You taught us the meaning of love by the way you loved our dad and I loved watching you tease each other. There was never a negative or disrespectful word uttered from your lips about our father even on the rare occasions when you disagreed.

You gave me the gift of music. The piano never rested in our home and the worn ivory keys were always grey from dirty little fingers as you patiently taught us to play. I loved the light I saw in your eyes every time you watched one of us perform at school or at church. No mother was more proud of her children.

Fame or fortune was never one of your

191

goals in life. You just made sure that there was the smell of freshly baked cinnamon rolls to greet us when we walked in the door from school. As you worked at home, cheerfully taking care of the same monotonous chores each day, you taught us to work and to find value in a job well done. There must have been days when you were tired or frustrated but all I remember is that our home was clean and dinner was always ready at 6 o'clock. Ten of us sat down to eat but you always jumped right back up to make sure we had everything we needed.

You loved beautiful things but seldom did you buy anything for yourself. I have never known anyone more selfless. All of your time and energy was given to us but that is what made you happy. From you I learned how to smile, how to laugh, and

how to be silly. I remember your boundless energy and optimism. Inside of you dwelt the spirit of a child; delighting in the little things in life that go unnoticed by most of us.

There were never any clubs or luncheons for you to go to. You didn't even drive a car until you were over fifty but you taught me how to be independent and told me that I could accomplish anything. I've grown up believing that there was nothing I couldn't do if I really tried. You gave me the gift of limitless possibilities in life.

One of your great loves was the mountains. Through you I learned to love hiking and to appreciate the beauty of a sunset. There was a reverence inside of you for God and all of his creations. You loved people and people loved you. Hundreds were there to mourn your passing and some of your friends still carry your picture in their wallets. You never understood what a difference you made each day in the lives of so many.

Since you passed away I've married a wonderful man, had three children, climbed mountains, and ran marathons. I've watched everything you instilled in us pass on to your grandchildren and great-grandchildren. You are with me every day. You're in the faces of my brothers and sisters as we reminisce about our childhood. You're in the kitchen with me every time I bake a batch of cookies. You're in the music I hear from my daughter's Viola. You've been with me on my runs and hikes. I see your smile in every sunrise and sunset. Your small life has made so many lives possible. Too many women look for acceptance from the world in the acknowledgment of their abilities and accomplishments. You quietly lived a simple life that will bless the lives of generations. I'm so grateful to be your daughter. I love you.

Clynn Mann
Engineer

As a young boy I always thought that people were taking advantage of my father. For that reason I saw him as weak. As I grew older and much wiser I came to realize that my father cared deeply for every one he met. He never passed a stalled automobile on the highway without checking to see if he could help in any way. If there was anyone in our neighborhood that had a need of any kind, he was there to help.

Mom and dad had wanted to go to Hawaii for many years and they had a special account that they had saved up for to pay for the trip. They had just about reached their goal, when they were assessed a large amount of money for a new chapel to be built in the area. My father paid his assessment and an equal amount extra, because he was sure that they were families that could not afford their share.

For many years he was a department manager of a local department store. The department had an entrance from the parking deck, and he spent a lot of time helping people start their cars or changing flat tires for those that could not do it themselves. During his years of the department store, he supervised a lot of different people. I never met a person that did not have a great fondness for him. I believe that my dad's ability to get along well with people was his greatest accomplishment. I only hope that I can live my life as well as he did his.

194

Jamie O'Hara Laurens
Writer, Creative Writing Teacher

COMPANIONS FOR WINIFRED ZEIGLER

I'm making an imprint in my mind so that twenty
or two years from now when you are gone I can carry
 a piece of your voice curled in my ear, scratched on my eyelids.
You've left your teacup empty
and half a cracker for me on the table by the lamp.

Half light through slatted screens catches
the easy way your feet glide into modern shoes, a glint
in your hair,
You are holding a magazine
propped in your lap like a misbehaving child,
pretending to read.

In just seconds
you break the silence we have worked to find
in the retreated corner of this evening.
I am delighted and neglect my paragraphs.

It's about a phone call made whenever,
the weather. How nice it is to be with family.
You say 'whenever' in that way uniquely yours
as if time, not counted on a clock, were to be given away.

195

I strain to capture your grasp on sounds, the silence between.
I wish to appear in my empty hands a paintbrush and a
perfect canvas
to capture these: I, I told her, you know.
It is magnificent, the minutiae of your voice.

You hug the magazine to your belly. I know before you do
that you will stroke it in a maternal way, like a blanket,
as if it were tender, this excuse to be quiet together.

I haven't let you read much, you say.
I don't want to read.
Then what I don't tell you surrounds my eyes, and props
up the jars of my ears.

My heart is heavy, my mind scrambles, hoping
wrapping memory like twine around the spindle
of this here and now will you let this voice
whisper wisdom from beyond,
An impossible wish, as memory's a trickster,
as however I engrave this scrap of your voice I
may have nothing left
but the trace of the shape of a sound,
its outline, illegitimate, created by memory.

Can I count on its quality, scratched like a record
your laugh softly trilled as if down so many pipes?
The glimmer of your eyes lit up so many ways
risks already to be replaced by a photograph of a moment
I didn't see.
Maybe I'll keep the imprint
of the pads of your fingers on my arm,
keep that in my pocket like a stone.

Vessel, uncapturable, fleeting the strokes of even a pen,
I should have tasted the cracker.

We are reluctant to go when we are called, so
we move at a limp, a bumbled two-step,
lips pressed with secrets. I'm smug
with this crowd, we didn't need them with their flowers and their wine,
We had half a cracker between us, and all the time of the world.

✳ ✳ ✳

"Companions" recounts an hour I spent with my grandmother. The opening stanza describes our real surroundings at that moment: we were in a room in the fading light of evening. She had a lamp on, and she had bitten into a cracker and offered me the rest. As I was writing the poem, I realized that this was also true of the way she has shown me how to live. She has shown me how to enjoy that which is given to us, even in something as small as a cracker. She has taught me that life is sweet, that it can be lived as simply as a song, and that every person we love, every day, every moment we live, is a gift. She has left the light on for me, and for that I'm grateful.

Shellie "Marie" Nielson
Homemaker

I was named after an amazing woman, Jane Marie Barlows. She was my Grandmother. When I was born the doctor said I probably would never be able to walk or maybe with a walker. I had severe club feet. My Grandmother had so much faith. She was a strong Catholic woman and she made a deal with God. She prayed and promised that if I would be able to walk she would never smoke cigarettes again. After many surgeries, casts and corrective braces on my legs as a child I can walk. I love my Nana. She was the funniest Grandmother. She would cuss up a storm, but she made me laugh. She would do Karate kicks and cartwheels. She was a hoot.

As my Grandparents got older my Grandfather got Alzheimer's disease. Nana took care of him for fifteen years through-out this horrible disease. At first she would care for him at home, but when he was no longer able to walk, he was too heavy for her to carry him so he had to be put into a hospital. My Grandmother would be at the hospital caring for him, feeding him EVERY DAY. The hospital was smelly and yucky, but she would be down there making the other patients laugh, telling jokes, being her funny self.

My Grandfather died and within one year Nana wasn't feeling well and found out she had bone cancer. (I believe Grandpa was calling her home with him.) She still had a sense of humor. She would say "I have the big C." After months of chemotherapy she lost most of her hair. When I would bring my two little boys over to visit Nana, she would surprise them and whip her wig off the top of her head and say

199

"Wheee." They would giggle. She died six months after my Grandfather.

Nana never stopped making me laugh. Her legacy leaves me with the knowledge that God is watching over me. He hears my prayers and He answers them. She taught me to have an attitude of optimism throughout my life. No matter what life deals me to always look on the sunny side.

At Home with Jackie Robinson

William "Scott" Fisher
Radio Broadcaster

The month following the passing of my father in April 1972 was among the most difficult in my life. Taken by a heart attack, Dad had been my good friend, counselor, and teacher. With just two months to go before high school graduation, he would not be there. And so my life had been effectively divided into two eras: my growing up years with my father always there, and everything after, without him.

The greatest interest we had shared was a love of baseball. He had grown up a fan of the New York Giants, as his father was before him. But with the Giants having moved on to San Francisco, our time was spent cheering for their National League successors in New York, the Mets. We followed them from their ridiculous beginnings as lovable losers to the America

World Series victory of 1969. Our "baseball bonding" was often highlighted by stories of the favorite Giant players of his youth . . . Carl Hubbell, Bill Terry, Freddie Fitzsimmons, and Mel Ott, as well as other greats he'd been privileged to watch, like Babe Ruth and Lefty Gomez of the Yankees, and, later, Jackie Robinson of the Brooklyn Dodgers. It didn't matter to Dad that Robinson had been a dreaded Dodger . . . and certainly not that he was black . . . Robinson had been a fearless ballplayer, and a fearless human being.

This foundation in baseball lore took hold early, and I started a rather modest collection of autographs of the great players of the past at the age of thirteen, often attending old-timers games in New York, and, in my mid-teens, Hall of Fame induction ceremonies in Cooperstown. I shared this budding interest with a friend from the other side of my hometown, Cos Cob, Connecticut. His name was David Zimmerman.

At eighteen, Dave was a year older than I, muscular and good-natured, and was mistakenly certain he himself would one day play in the major leagues. He was the picture of teenage confidence, and I, more timid, was often happy to allow him to pave the way for both of us. We were equally awed by the legends we pursued, but Dave would not allow himself to show it.

About a month after my father's passing, Dave came by the house to visit. I was still coping with my loss, and doing allI could to complete the studies necessary for my graduation, when my redheaded friend suggested we go on another of our autograph hunting adventures.

"You've got to get out of here for a while," Dave said. "I found out where

Jackie Robinson lives!"

My mood instantly changed. Dave had my full attention. Robinson was not only a baseball icon, but a symbol of courage worldwide for having endured the overwhelming challenges of breaking baseball's color barrier in 1947. To a young man growing up in the '60s and '70s, Jackie Robinson represented all the reasons that people everywhere should want to support the fight for equality.

Dave's plan to drop in on Jackie Robinson created a bit of a dilemma for me, however. As bad as I was feeling about things at the time, the idea that I might be firmly asked to immediately leave by a man I considered a hero, was almost more than I could bear. Nonetheless, I relented. But I convinced Dave that I thought it was important that we both wear a jacket and tie so that he might know we were being as respectful as possible for a couple of imposing teenagers.

When the selected day arrived, Dave picked me up in his beat up, white, 66 Dodge Dart. With him, to my surprise, was a mutual friend.

"Tom wanted to come, too!" Dave smiled. Without betraying my fear that there were now too many on this "mission" for it to possibly succeeds, I hopped in. With me, I carried a pen and the last Christmas gift Dad had given me, "This Great Game," a picture book of the standout players of all time, including of course, Jackie Robinson. Dad had inscribed it just five months before, "Merry Christmas 1971 To Scott, my favorite fan, Love, Dad."

We made our way through the winding roads of the Connecticut backwoods to the Merritt Parkway and headed north to neighboring Stamford. Dave confidently negotiated the route without hesitation.

Clearly, he had made a rehearsal run.

Twenty minutes into our journey, Dave slowed down as he approached a driveway on the right. I still remember my first view of the Robinson home, down the lane and through the trees, where the driveway ended in a circle. I was struck by how private a home it was. Surely, Jackie Robinson wasn't going to like our intrusion. I swallowed as we opened the car doors, gathered our treasures, stepped out and adjusted our ties.

As we approached the front door, I began to hear the pumping of my own heart. "It's not too late to turn back!" I thought to myself. Instinctively, I walked behind Dave as he purposefully made his way to the front porch and, without hesitation, rang the doorbell. I could barely hear the sound of the approaching footsteps over my increasingly loud heart.

We heard a fumble with the lock; saw

the handle move and the door crack open all of about six inches. "Yes?" A female voice asked as its owner peered around the door.

"We're here to see Mr. Robinson!" Dave confidently announced.

"Just a moment, please," responded the voice as the door slammed in our faces.

We didn't say a word as we stood there waiting for what was probably about two minutes, but seemed like a solid hour. I chewed anxiously on my lower lip, hoping for the best, but anticipating that the great Mr. Robinson would probably not appreciate a visit from three strangers interrupting his day.

When the door opened again, Rachel Robinson, Jackie's wife, smiled and said, "He'll see you in the living room!"

The camera in my mind began to roll. "You can never forget this!" I thought. "Remember EVERYTHING!" Walking through the door. Long hall. Straight to the back. Down three steps. Wrought iron railing. Sunken living room.

A voice brought us out of our stupor. "What can I do for you, boys?" asked Jackie Robinson. Our heads snapped to the right to find the diamond great seated comfortably on a couch, almost like a regular mortal, but we knew he was certainly not that. To his right, in a nearby chair was a guest, an African-American man of about seventy. We saw that Robinson had invited us in, fully aware we would interrupt his visit with this man.

"We'd like you to sign some things for us," our spokesman announced.

"Sure," agreed Jackie. He introduced us to his guest and invited us to make ourselves at home. "Sit down over here."

Dave, Tom, and I crowded around him on the sofa, as the former Dodger carefully signed his very legible signature to every item we brought. In the book my father had given me, by a picture of second baseman saving a pennant with a diving catch, he wrote," To Scott, Best Wishes, Jackie Robinson."

As we thanked him for his many kindnesses, he stood up and smiled as we shook his hand.

Our trip back to Cos Cob was loud and joyous. "Wait until my mother hears our story of how Jackie Robinson invited us into his home!" And, "Wait 'til our friends see those autographs." For a man undoubtedly hounded by fans throughout his life, the thought that he would make time to greet three boys in his living room was beyond belief. Jackie Robinson was no longer a character in a remarkable story about social progress and equal rights for all. He was . . . a Friend!

That visit occupied many of my thoughts over the next few weeks, and it hurt that I couldn't share the story with my father. I spend a portion of my last days at Greenwich high in the school library reading up on the story of this remarkable man, and looking at the writing in my treasured book from both Jackie Robinson, and my father.

Shortly after my graduation, while rummaging through some old magazines in an antique store, I ran across a 1955 Brooklyn Dodgers scorecard, from the only year Jackie Robinson's team had ever won a World Series. It was an expensive seven dollars, but I had to have it.

I showed it to Dave soon after. "Wish I had had this when we went to Jackie Robinson's house," I lamented.

"Well, let's go back!" replied Dave.

I vainly protested the idea that we would repeat our intrusion. Dave said that he and Tom would go without me then. So, hesitantly, I agreed to go along.

205

On our return visit, Jackie Robinson himself came to the door. It had only been six weeks since we have seen him, but his appearance shocked us. The whites of his eyes were yellow, and he wasn't looking directly at us as he had done previously.

"Put the pen where you would like me to sign, boys. I don't see too well anymore."

We silently obliged, and he slowly wrote his name for each of us, again, including the lineup portion of my scorecard. We thanked him one more time, and quietly drove off, taken back by the noticeably deteriorating health of our obliging hero.

Summer turned to autumn, and I began my first year of studies as a Communications major at Ithaca College in upstate New York. I remember watching television coverage of the World Series between Cincinnati and Oakland. Before the

second game, everyone rose to applaud the ceremonial throwing out of the first pitch by one Jack Roosevelt Robinson. He waved to acknowledge the cheers of the Cincinnati fans, and I smiled to see that he was still well enough to inspire all he came in contact with.

Only nine days later, on October 24th, 1972 . . . six months to the day after my father's death . . . the world was shocked to hear the news of his passing. At only fifty years of age, heart disease, as a complication of diabetes, had taken the life of Jackie Robinson, one of baseball's greatest stars, and one of America's most influential figures.

Over the next several days, news programs broadcast grainy black and white films of the young, pigeon-toed baseman racing from third base to steal home, knocking home runs, and celebrating championships. Aging former teammates spoke of what he had brought to the Dodgers. Testimonials were given as to the meaning his life and example had brought to Americans of color. White Americans expressed praise for the man who had made them more aware of the plight of their black neighbors. And countless African-Americans shed tears over their most grievous loss. Jackie Robinson had deeply impacted many people.

My sadness on this occasion was tempered with gratitude. The pictures in my mind were markedly different from those on television, and certainly fresher and clearer.

The white-haired, middle-aged Jackie Robinson, while weak in body, had on two occasions taken the time to greet three young boys. And, in my case, he had brought me the greatest moments of happiness I had experienced since the passing of my father. He had been kind enough to invite us into his home. He had been thoughtful enough to visit with us again at his doorstep when he could barely see. Dad's old stories of Jackie's exploits had changed from storybook status to real life. In his last six months, Jackie Robinson had personally touched my life, just as he had so many millions of other Americans throughout his. And just as he continues to inspire lives today, over thirty years since his passing.

Cameron M.
Software Engineer

Once a wise man said, "the meaningful moments in life are far and few between and most of them end before they start." As I have grown older and have seen the ups and downs in my life, I have realized that wisdom can be measured when the sum of ones accumulative experiences gives the ability to know these moments, capture them, live them to the fullest, and cherish them long after they have ended. These experiences come as gifts and most of them seem to be unexpected. Those unexpected moments, if captured with open heart and mind are the ones that make lasting impressions and make life worth living.

I had a normal childhood in a middle-class family growing up in Iran with experiences not unlike most children in the Western world. Same hopes of growing up to be a scientist, astronaut, or maybe the doctor that finds the cure for cancer, hopes of growing up to be a man that can make a difference in the world as a human being. Little did I know that about the time I was coming of age a set of events transpired in Iran that was labeled by the rest of the world as the so-called Islamic Revolution. It turned our world upside down. Our normal lives turned into a living hell and our normal concerns and expectations were replaced with daily striving for survival in a world that seemed to be built on an iceberg which suddenly started to melt under our feet.

All those simple pleasures that are taken for granted everywhere else in the free world were taken away from the lives of every Iranian. What I used to hear on the news about the "Killing Fields of Cam-

208

bodia, or "Streets of Beirut" became daily occurrences in Iran. Every day became a horrifying episode of a never-ending horror show. The universities were closed; people were being fired from their jobs for not being religious. The ongoing witch-hunt kept taking its toll on innocent Iranian people. It continues to this day.

Living through those trying times made me question all of my beliefs, everything I had been taught since I was a child. How could there be a divine justice when there are humans capable of such atrocities while the whole world looks the other way. Saadi, one of the most famous sports and philosophers in Iran's history once wrote: "All of Adams children are like the complimentary parts of one living being, and they have all been created of the same fabric, once one part is in pain, the whole body will become restless." It seems that many of us have amnesia and we've forgotten how we are related and our similarities far exceed our cosmetic differences. In our forgetfulness we hurt others or turn a blind eye to wrongdoings in our presence. Living through times like that is unfortunate, but if we manage to gain focus and remember to listen to our inner voice or conscience we start seeing some people that shine in the middle of all the darkness that surrounds them. They are like beacons of hope to help and guide others and set an example, to remind us that our nature is goodness and light and not darkness. Those peoples' purpose is to guide us in our destined paths. I was fortunate enough to start recognizing these beacons of light in my path early on.

In those trying times around 1981 be-

209

fore the universities closed in Iran I met the girl that changed my life forever and became my wife and my companion in life and eternity. When I met her for the first time I was overcome by the strange and pleasant feeling that I had known her all my life. I had that feeling before knowing who she was, and everything up to that moment was a buildup and movement in that direction. After that moment I felt that I aged years and matured overnight. In a subconscious way I woke up from a long slumber. However, the process of waking up did not stop there and continued for years after that. She taught me new ways of looking at things, events and people and guided me in the right direction.

Though we were young, we decided that for building a life and living our childhood dreams we could not stay in condi-tions without hope, purpose or future. So we decided to escape from Iran and head toward the free world and start our lives there. My father and my brother escaped out of the country shortly before then. They had left through the southern part of Azerbaijan into Turkey with the help of Iranian Kurds that knew my father from his days of being a commanding officer of the Iranian army in that region. After several months, my father called us from America and told us the story of the hardships and dangers they had endured on their journey. Hearing their story made it clear that with the war between Iran and Iraq on that side of the country, and with governments of Iran and Turkey having the border between the countries under tight surveillance there was no way to leave in that direction. On the eastern side there was a war between Afghans and the Soviets occupying their country; Iran's government was controlling the border with Pakistan closely to prevent people from escaping the country using that route. During that period all legal means of leaving Iran were blocked by the government, but we were powered by hope, driven by the energy of youth, and ready to die if it meant freedom from the life we were living. The sequence of events in the months that followed and the people that came our way all guided us through a dangerous journey that led us to freedom and a new life in America. Looking back it seems that the minor details are sketchy but I remember everything, and it unfolds in my head like a dream, and sometimes I ask myself was it really us that did all of that?

In passing and by accident I mentioned our plan to escape Iran to a neighbor. There was no explanation for what we did because it defied any sense of reason but somehow we did that as if it was meant to be. The neighbor was my friend's father and his demeanor always make you think twice before wanting to say anything more than exchange greetings. But for some unknown reason he came our way and one thing led to another. As it turned out he was the chief of a tribe in the central plains and held the ceremonial leadership position in his tribe, but he lived in Tehran with his two sons. He told us that he had a friend, a Mr. K., in the South Eastern province of Baluchistan and that the friend was one of the tribal chiefs there and could probably help us escape. As we realized later, in American terminology Mr. K. was the "Godfather" figure in that area and had

211

a hand in almost everything that was illegal. We met him at our neighbor's house. He was a middle-aged, dark skinned heavyset man with a Baluchee accent and a commanding presence. Even now, looking back, I can't believe that we came in contact with such a person, a man that could create fear in you with just the sound of his voice. He explained the process of leaving through the desert across the border and the dangers involved in that. His concern was not the border patrol because he claimed that most of them knew him and were afraid of him or were on his payroll. On the contrary, he was worried about crossing paths with other drug-lord's convoys that could end up in a shoot-out. I believe that our neighbor noticed that Mr. K. was instilling fear in us and it seemed that he was beginning to worry about his

friend putting us in harm's way, so he intervened, and asked a series of questions to see what sort of security his friend was going to provide for us. Mr. K. promised that his men would protect us at all costs, but our neighbor was not convinced that he could trust his men and started talking about the importance of honoring their friendship and the need for him to do more. Finally Mr. K. promised to send his own son across with us for protection to make our neighbor happy.

We had lived across the street from our neighbor for several years only exchanging pleasantries in passing and not really knowing what kind of person he was, and now he was doing anything in his power to help us escape and was trying hard to negotiate our safety as if we were more than neighbors to him.

In the short time that followed my wife and I got married and started our life together just a few weeks before our escape. We spent those days making the necessary preparations. One of the hardest things I have ever done and witnessed was to say goodbye and bid farewell to my family and watch my wife do the same with her parents. For the longest time I could not fathom the measure of understanding that my wife's parents had toward our love for each other and what we were about to do. Only now that I am older and have my own children do I understand what her parents must have felt and gone through.

When the time came our neighbor flew to Baluchistan with us and stayed at his friends home while we awaited the time to leave. He promised to stay there until we called him from the other side and assured him of our safety. Traveling inside Iran was not easy. One had to go through many security checks and inspections on the way, and had to provide justification for travel to the people at the airport and at every step of the way.

When we arrived in Zabol, a city near the border of Afghanistan, Mr. K. was at the airport and took us, (our neighbor, my mother, my wife, and me,) to his house. His family was very hospitable and we stayed with them for a couple of days. We couldn't tell if they knew the reason why we were there, so during our stay we did not talk about that at all. We were filled with fear and excitement at the same time. Fear of what was ahead of us, and excitement about the possibility of living free again. A couple of days later they took us to his ranch that was literary on the border of Iran and Afghanistan. There we waited for the right conditions to leave. Our wait was not more than a day but that must have been one of the longest days I have lived through.

The fateful moment arrived on a moonlight night on the last week of March in 1983. Since we did not speak the local dialect and were not as dark-skinned as the local people, we were told to stay out of sight and not call attention to ourselves. Finally the wait was over and it was time to go. A pick-up truck was loaded with food, water, some light weapons, and ammunition. There was my wife and I, along with my mother, Mr. K's son as the driver, a guard to protect us, and a guide to direct us. We shook hands with our neighbor and promised to call him as soon as we could, then we started heading eastbound across a narrow river. I was sitting in the back of the pickup along with the guard and the guide, and my wife and my mother in the front next to the driver. This was the last time we were on Iranian soil, the country where we were born.

As soon as we were across the border they turned the cars headlights off and started driving in the desert where there was no road. The only source of light was the full moon, and the guide would correct the driver's directions every so often by looking at the constellations in the night sky. We were going through Afghanistan because the border there was not controlled as much as in Pakistan due to the war raging in that country. Iran's government had figured that nobody would be crazy enough to try and escape using that route.

During that nightmare-like night we passed old battlefields with destroyed vehicles littered across the desert, and numerous abandoned villages that turned into ghost towns after the villagers escaped to safety in Iran or Pakistan. The car broke down before dawn in the middle of nowhere. The driver spent a couple of hours until he managed to fix the truck. Those hours felt like eternity. I could hear the guide and the guard talking to each other and I understood some of what they were saying. They were concerned because there was a town about thirty kilometers east from where we were and apparently there had been heavy fighting between the Soviets and the Afghan rebels only days before. In daylight we were exposed and if the planes spotted us on the ground they could blow us away by mistaking us for Afghan fighters. After we started moving again it took us until noon before we crossed into Pakistan. During those hours before the crossing when we were driving in the desert I was fixated on the horizon. I was waiting in fear for Soviet Migs to appear but we were lucky and nothing happened. After we were finally out of the danger zone I could relax a little and just sit in the hot sun looking at the desert landscape while we crossed numerous sand dunes. Finally we got on some unpaved road. The rest of the day we drove deeper into Pakistan. Once, in the late afternoon the driver got off the road and drove into bushes on a nearby dry river bed and told us to be quiet. Before long we saw a convoy going in the opposite direction, it looked like another drug lord's crew heading home to Baluchistan. After twenty-four hours we arrived at a safe house and spent the night there. The next morning Mr. K.'s son hired a Pakistani driver with a pickup truck to take us to Quetta. He told us that his mission was over and bid us farewell.

We arrived at the destination that night. There was martial law in Pakistan at the time, which meant that in every village or town we had to stop at checkpoints. My wife and my mother were given Burkas to wear on top of their clothes and I was wearing a Pakistan loose pajamas type outfit on top of my jeans. Once we arrived at Quetta our fears were mostly over. The driver took us to a house of an Iranian family that had lived there for a long time. These people were also contacts of Mr. K. They helped us get tickets to Karachi and notified their contacts to help us leave the country from there.

From Quetta we made phone calls back to Iran and America to let our families know of our safe arrival. We also called our former neighbor and thanked him for everything he had done for us. I remember hearing his sigh of relief.

From Karachi we flew to Zurich, Switzerland. We spent less than two weeks there until we secured our visas to the United States. During our time in Zurich we marveled at how freely people lived, moved around, dressed and acted without fear of persecution.

We arrived in New York on April 15, 1983. I was trying to see the New York skyline from the window while the airplane was circling the airport before getting permission to land. I was familiar with the New York skyline from movies and pictures, but it was overcast that day and there was nothing to see. When the captain finally announced preparations for the final approach I looked out the window again, and suddenly through an opening in the clouds I saw Ellis Island and the Statue of Liberty standing there with the torch in her hands looking towards the horizon. I realized that she was lighting the way for people like us that were forced out of their homes and were in search of freedom and a second chance in life. What I especially noticed were her feet. There were broken chains on them to symbolize her as one of us, someone who had to break the chains in order to break free and then she would stand there as an angel to light the way for the rest of us that would be coming over time. In a few moments she disappeared as suddenly as she had appeared to greet us and there was nothing left but clouds. Once a wise man said that, "the meaningful moments in life are so far and few in between and most of them end before they start."

Now, years later, I reflect upon all of those experiences, and remember how one stranger, a neighbor, crossed our path and changed our lives forever. How he helped us on every step of the way to guarantee our safety in our quest for freedom. Talking to him from Quetta was the last time we heard his voice and after that we lost him and could not find him in Iran again, but we remember him. Our ordeal ended there and our life here began, but I can't ever forget that Iranian people have been living in worsening condition ever since with no hope in sight.

Phillip Collins
British Satirist/Writer

In the early fifties, I lived for every other Saturday afternoon, during the long winter football (soccer) season. On those days, which never seemed to arrive, my father would drive us thirteen miles to see Portsmouth football club (chairman: Viscount Montgomery of El Alemein) play the Beautiful Game. Opponents came from such exotic places as Bolton, Cardiff and Preston (North End).

The drive, through the gray, the wind and rain, sleet and snow, fog and ice was a lengthy pre-prelude to the more enjoyable prelude of shuffling through the Fratton Park gates. An hour early, and at my insistence, to drink in the atmosphere, watch the crowd arrive, and enjoy a steaming cup of pre-match Bovril. Magic time. Ninety nine percent of the crowd were home-grown, back then. Dyed in the wool Pompey supporters. The Pompey Chimes: "Play up Pompey! . . . Pompey play up!" Very few visiting supporters, so no crowd violence, since there was no one to bash. Ergo, peace in our time.

The program, sixpence, identified the players from both teams, and those who had represented their country had a small E (England), I (Ireland), S (Scotland) or W (Wales) against their name. My pride bubbled when, more often than not, I saw that every Portsmouth player was an international. Around 1954, sides varied little from week to week, so my band of heroes was pretty constant, and injury would have to be pushing fatal to see a player unable to continue. There were no substitutes. Ninety minutes of heroics.

Fratton Park was the hub of a working-class residential neighborhood. Access to the South Stand, where we sat, was at the end of a terraced street with a pub on a corner, some twenty five yards from the ground's imposing main gates.

Arriving later than usual, one freezing Saturday, we saw a man emerge from the pub, flick a lighted cigarette into the gutter and head for he grounds. He toted a shoulder bag, from which a pair of football boots dangled by their laces.

My father gave me a hefty nudge and said, "Look, it's Norman Uprichard . . . " And there he was. Much taller than I imagined. The Irish international and Portsmouth goalkeeper. The Keeper between the sticks. The miracle man who punched, parried, deflected or caught most of the shots that Great Britain's finest could fire at him. My dad hastily produced a pen and his checkbook (the first piece of paper to hand), and I rushed up to Norman and asked him for his autograph. He looked at me and without breaking a stride, said, "Bug off."

Football was never quite the same after that.

219

Doris S. Platt
Compiler

*I*n the late forties and early fifties, the Red Cross placed many children from the war-torn countries of Europe with Swiss families, there to be restored to physical, mental, and emotional health. I was fortunate to be among those who benefited from the generosity of the Swiss people. After a long train journey, I reached the small village of Malix, a few mountain ranges from the resort town of St. Moritz. Here Peter and Ursula Hassler welcomed me into their home.

Mrs. Hassler had a comfortable, easy-going personality. She was responsible for the running of the household and made sure I took baths and always had clean clothing. An excellent cook, she invariably worried that I ate too little.

To his surprise, the sterner Mr. Hassler became my hero. Ruth and Helen, the couple's two teenaged daughters, were away at boarding school. Their absence made me the fortunate, sole recipient of their father's attention. Being the village headmaster, he was well used to children's questions and answered my endless inquiries with unequaled patience. Soon I followed him like a shadow.

I called him Papa and tried to match the length of my strides to his. When he took me shopping and bought a smaller version of his boots with identical markings on the soles, I was absolutely sure no child anywhere could be happier.

A tall man with aquiline features, Papa had salt-and-pepper hair and a dignified bearing. He was a man of keen knowledge born of study and introspection. Comfortable with his thoughts and his mountains, he deeply appreciated nature and her creations.

His profound understanding of quiet and gentle things found expression in the practical realities of his life. In addition to teaching school, Papa kept bees, several milk cows, pigs, goats, chickens, and a large Belgian draft horse called Norma.

The bees occupied quite a bit of his time. When he spun honey out of the combs, he let me eat all the amber nectar I wanted. I quickly learned there could be too much of a good thing, another lesson that by *doing,* we begin to *know.*

My daily chores included feeding the chickens, keeping the kitchen wood box filled, and holding the tails of the cows while Papa milked each one. He made me feel as if those were the most important jobs anyone could have.

In early summer, residents of Malix moved to their chalets in the high meadows, taking with them some household goods and the livestock. Most of the cattle were taken onto the alp, higher yet.

From early morning until late in the afternoon, I watched, fascinated, as Papa cut the aromatic grass with long, rhythmic sweeps of his scythe. In two or three weeks, when the grass had been cut, dried, and safely stored in a barn, we moved to another chalet and repeated the whole process.

It was an idyllic Heidi-type of life, a school of trees and starlight, complete with green hills to roam and cozy haylofts for my friends and me to sleep in. At night, the last sounds I heard before drifting off to sleep were the rich-toned bells of the cows and the more silvery ones of the goats.

Papa showed me how to find my way in the forest, which mushrooms were safe to eat and which were poisonous, how to understand the habits of various animals, and how to tell time by where the sun stood in the sky. Yet of all he taught me, his love of learning has been the most enriching.

I remember him as being a dedicated student of history and an avid reader of the classics, professional journals, and the newspaper—the last, preferably without interruption. In the evening after the chores were done, he invariably asked, "So, what did you learn today?"

My answers were seldom to his satisfaction.

"That's it? That's it?" he would demand.

"Well, that's all I can think of."

On the heels of my response came his quick, insistent, "That is not enough! I want you to live as if every day is your last—as if every minute is your last! I want you to see and feel and think! Absorb and digest! If you learn something on Wednesday and you don't know any more on Friday, it means Thursday had nothing to say."

According to Papa, surface thinking used only the outer layers of the mind. Because he saw more clearly and thought more deeply, he found everything worthy of his attention. Little escaped him. Knowledge was a carrier of truth; learning, not a chore or an obligation, but a joyous pursuit. His example created in me a constant desire to ask the why of things.

Papa's influence continued to be felt years later in the lives of my own children. Because of him, the so-called price of admission to our family's evening meal was the sharing of one item of knowledge each of us had discovered that day. And it could not be anything warmed over. My daughters would diligently come to the table with their newfound nuggets; my son often made last-minute sprints to the encyclopedia for his.

Now, years later, it pleases me to see all of them passing on this love for learning to their children. I think Papa would be pleased, as well.

222

On the 5th of November I was in a hotel room in Show Low, Arizona, checking my phone messages. I had a rare call from my younger brother, who hates to use the phone. The message went something like this: "Matt, this is Rod. Something has happened. Call me." I knew it was serious. When I finally reached my brother, he told me that Denise, a friend from my youth, had just committed suicide. The shocking news left me searching in vain for something to say. I tried to put it out of my thoughts, but it would not leave me. I was sad that night and for a long time thereafter. Denise was the first girl I had dated. She was the first love of my life. More than that, she was a lifeline that helped guide me through those turbulent teenage years. Having been born in the late 1950s, I missed the "liberating" 1960s; rather, I grew up in the aftermath.

Going to high school in California's Bay Area in the 1970s was no easy task for a young man who had been taught to live a moral and clean life, but who was faced with any number of temptations every day. A friend of mine regularly boasted of his sexual escapades. I knew from listening to others that his behavior was not unique. Pornography was easy to come by, though not as easy as it is today with the Internet. Alcohol, cigarettes, and drugs were prevalent. And worst of all, it was considered "cool' to be involved in all of these things. In some way, it almost seemed necessary to do so just to fit in.

I realize now that many adults have struggles avoiding the kind of things that distract, addict, and eventually lead to self-destruction, but these insights come with adult perspective.

At that crucial juncture in my life, just

223

as I was confronting a multitude of mixed and confusing messages, there came into my life a girl who lived a higher standard. This was Denise. She came from a religious family and she took her faith seriously. She was not self-righteous or condescending about it; rather, she simply lived her beliefs. I asked her out several times and before I knew it, I was in love.

When I was with Denise, I was aware of her moral standard and her great expectations of me. These inspired me to be on my best behavior. My thoughts and actions naturally elevated to a higher level because of her influence. This feeling lingered when we were apart so that I did my best to live the standard she expected. Were I to do the opposite, I knew I would have felt very uncomfortable in her presence; it would have ruined the friendship.

Denise and I dated from the time we were sixteen until she left for college and I went away on a two-year service assignment. While I was gone, Denise got married. After that, I did not see much of her. In fact, I have rarely seen her in the last twenty-seven years. But the sweet memories persist. I know that I was inspired by her goodness to make good decisions, decisions that have had long-lasting consequences.

I am still pained and puzzled at what caused her to take her life. I am very sad when I think of the desperation that drove her to such a drastic action. However, the influence she had on me has remained and has blessed my life ever since. She is a person I will never forget. I wish I had told her all of this before she died.

Doris S. Platt
Compiler

Sentinels, or examples in our lives, help us stretch the definition of what is possible. One of those learning moments came when I listened to the dialogue between a TV reporter and a guest, a man in a wheelchair who lives with spinal muscular atrophy. Steve Mikita was eighteen month old when physicians told his parents that he would not live to see his second birthday. Doctors voiced another opinion after his fourth birthday, saying he would not live long. Now aged forty-four, Mr. Mikita, assistant attorney general, adjunct professor of law, and popular motivational speaker, has written the story of his life in a book titled *The Third Opinion*. That opinion, full of hope and determination, is his own. Mr. Mikita's physical condition makes him totally dependent on others for the simplest of tasks. Yet, throughout the interview, I sensed in him no bitterness, nothing of the victim. Although his body continues to weaken, his will to live and his love for life grows ever stronger. He credits his parents for shaping his positive attitude. They could not teach him to walk, but they taught him to climb mountains.

"There is little I can do to control my body's deterioration," he stated. "The only things I can control are my reactions to it and my perspective of it. The key to our happiness is to appreciate and develop our strengths, not pity ourselves because we have weaknesses. We must learn to love and value ourselves for who we are, not hate ourselves for who we aren't. Ultimately, we are responsible for our happiness and our lives."

When Mr. Mikita was asked what he

225

would wish for if any of his desires could be granted, I listened with increased interest. Would this man, who had never walked, wish to run, dance, drive a car, or really climb that mountain? Would he wish to do the thousand things he surely must have thought about during endlessly challenging days and nights?

The answer was not something I had expected. "I would like to be able to kneel when I pray," he said.

I sat stunned. The innermost yearning of this man, who by necessity has to be concerned about navigating every moment of his life, was how to express gratitude to His Maker. On days when I feel pressured by my own burdens, his quiet example finds its way into my thoughts.

The opportunity of choice brought on by struggle and pain has reached deep into my soul to ask a simple life altering question. What will you do? The answer to that question has brought a joy I did not know was possible.

My wife's illness brought for a time great trials and heartache. Friends, family, and others would often ask, "Why do you stay? You can leave any time. Your life could be so much better. What will you do?"

My wife's commitment to survive and learn about life taught me the answer. I found choosing to learn all I could, accepting challenges as they were, and realizing that power of choice, (not blind acceptance), would result in personal strength I had never known before.

Life's challenges come regularly, many with new, unforeseen or unanticipated endings. Most arrive whether I like it or not, but as someone said, "Bring it on."

I now know what I will do. "Action, doing, and choosing" instead of passively sitting back and suffering, will move me to a better, happier place.

Trials and heartache have become the most powerful, positive influence on me and my family. Struggle is a friend I do not seek out, but embrace with choice when it arrives at the door.

227

John D. Gilfillan
Truck Sales Professional

I was recently asked what person or persons had influenced me the most. Having traveled a great deal and having met many, many people from all walks of life it took only a moment to answer, "My father." A simple man who really had life figured out in my estimation.

He and my mother raised thirteen children. That was impressive enough, since my father was a railroad conductor and was gone for days or weeks at a time. He didn't have much time to spend with each child and had to be shared by all of us. But he did teach us about honesty, love and loyalty. "Be convinced of your beliefs and stand tall for them. Be kind towards others, loyal to those who employ you, and honest to your friends and family." He used to say, "You will have many acquaintances and if you're lucky a handful of friends."

His love for his family was enormous. At my parent's wedding anniversary, (there were over three hundred people present), someone asked my father about his goals in life. His answer brought tears to my eyes. He smiled and said, "To have all of my children love each other."

228

My mom has been the greatest inspiration in my life. She has a wonderful heart, always thinking of herself last, if at all. When she was only six months old her mother died, when she was fourteen her father died. She then went to live with her Aunt, who was wonderful to her and taught her how to be a great person. The Aunt died when my mom was eighteen years old and away on vacation.

Despite all the hardships my mom endured—family loss and the Great Depression—she overcame it all. She got married to her only love, my dad, but after nineteen years of marriage and five children, he just left her. I was twelve at the time and didn't really think how hard it must be on her. I never heard her say," Why me?" not even once. Like always, she pulled herself up and kept us together. She gave us a nice home full of love and great childhood memories. My mom taught us that no matter how hard it is, just look around and you'll see someone worse off. She never had self-pity. She was always too busy giving of herself.

I'm sure she must have cried, but never around us. And she never allowed anyone to say negative things about my father. Some people tried, but she wouldn't have it, because "he is still your father." Because of her, I was able to forgive him.

When I got married and started having children of my own, I often thought that if I had had all that to overcome I would probably be a wreck. But when I stop and think of my sweet mom and all that she taught me through her words and more importantly her examples, I like to think I would be strong like her and make it. I am

229

so thankful to God for blessing me with such a special mom who taught us that it doesn't matter how little you may have, you can always help others in need. And that God will always be there for you, no matter what life has in store. I love my mom with my heart and soul and know when her time here is through; she'll be an angel in heaven continuing to show us the way. I am a good mom to my three beautiful daughters because of my special mom and her love. May God bless her.

Miguel M. Castroman
Physician Recruiter

This story begins in Uruguay, a small country in the southern part of South America. As in most of the region, the passion of the people is sports like soccer and local bicycle races. Accompanied by the cultural drink of mate, people always get together to discuss local sports events, and to listen to the radio. Here, in this country known for its passion for the tango and mate, where the gaucho can still be seen on the pampas, a young man grew up in humble circumstances. Since he was a little boy, he had developed a special interest for riding bicycles and participating in the local races.

In one of his first events, he rode a regular old bicycle, with heavy black tires, and a heavy frame. Most of the other competitors with their sports models didn't think he had a chance, but he proved them wrong and ended up the winner. He liked racing so much that he was determined to buy his own bicycle. His parents didn't have enough money, so he took a job delivering milk. Once he had saved enough he was able to buy the bicycle of his dreams, with ten gears and a much lighter frame.

He became a well-respected man, in sports and in person, and went on to win many races. He trained every day and became a local hero in the small town of Flores, Uruguay. But he didn't know that the biggest race of all was yet to come. While in his early 30s, with a wife and three children, he was diagnosed with cancer. He underwent numerous operations which at the beginning looked promising. It was at this time in his life, when an opportunity presented itself to move to Germany from where his wife was originally. The race for health started all over again. More surgeries, more pain, more patience were the trials he faced, but the cancer seemed to be winning. He tried every possible diet, workout, chemotherapy and much more. Finally the doctors gave up on him. This was a tough race. He knew he was leaving his wife and his children behind and there was nothing he or anybody else could do.

Throughout this time of pain and hopelessness, there was one thing nobody could take away from him. That one thing was his smile. He never made anyone feel sorry for how sick he was. He never stopped making jokes while the pain afflicted him. He never stopped telling jokes and remembering the good times.

Even in this state, when he was bedridden and the once quick legs that had propelled him to win could now barely carry him, people would gather like the multitudes that used to cheer him. He had the amazing ability to make others feel important about who they were. He would make them feel good about themselves. His smile and endurance were messages everybody appreciated.

With all the races he had won, one would think he lost this one. On the contrary, he gave a victory to everybody who knew him; the victory of being happy in life, no matter what the circumstances are; the victory of never giving up, never letting your circumstances bring you down, but enduring to the end.

This man was my father, and his life was a message I will never forget. Life is a race, but we're all winners, if at the end we still have that smile, the smile of a champion.

The Sentinel in my life is my Grandma. Not that my parents, or Grandpa for that matter weren't major influences, but Grandma was different.

My Grandma Ruth Hale taught me early on the importance of dreaming, and dreaming big. She used to say, "Life is too precious not to approach each day with a dream in mind." Not surprisingly, her life played out like a dream.

She always dreamed of being onstage. She and my Grandpa, Nathan Hale, worked hard at raising a young family in a small town in Utah. Both were proficient at writing stage plays, and both spent time onstage performing their own shows.

One day my Grandpa came home from the Copper Mine and said that he was tired of working each day at something he didn't love. My Grandma asked him if he had a dream, what would it be? He told her he wanted to move to Hollywood and become an actor. She said, "Then pack the car and we'll go." And they did.

After several months of attempting to pierce the Hollywood veil without luck, Grandma resolved that if nobody was going to hire them to act in their shows, she was going to write her own. That was the beginning of over three decades of writing, producing and acting onstage.

Today, the Hale Center Theater is the longest-running theater group in America. Grandma penned close to one hundred plays, founded five theaters, and left a legacy which proved that dreams do come true.

On a personal note, when I graduated

233

from film school (I kind of always knew I would end up in the industry on some level), my Grandma gave me the media screen rights to all of her stage plays. It is now my dream to take some of her work to another medium. If there's one sentinel in my life who proved that reality is only a dream away . . . it's Grandma.

I come from a long line of teachers. They stand on the road of my life as I look back, each at a formative moment, each one nudging me further down the paths I took, and the choices I made. These teachers are more than memories, and more than mentors. They taught me, corrected me, pushed me, punished me, encouraged me, defined me, and created the person I am now. I loved teachers because they were family first: my dad, Mr. Keddington, everyone's favorite science teacher, and my grandfather, Mr. McDonald, scholar and Irish storyteller. With a love and respect for teachers a part of me from my earliest days, I looked to other teachers readily for instruction and experience.

Kindergarten—the land of graham crackers and milk, nap blankets and recess, and the first of many special teachers in my life. Mrs. Picket was patient, soft spoken, and kind. But one day she asked me to stay after school. I was filled with a five year old's fear of discipline, wondering what I had done wrong, hoping she hadn't noticed me kicking Patrick Neff in the shins early that day. She opened my workbook and asked me to explain the assignment I had completed, why had I circled the pictures I had? I pointed to the crown, the rose, the fairy, the unicorn, the mermaid, the princess, the pony, and the kitten. They were all beautiful and I thought it was more fun to circle those pictures than the boring ones that had the dubious merit of starting with the letter "J". She explained how glad she was that I

235

loved beautiful things. She told me seeing beauty is a gift and such vision will make me a happy person. But, to be a well-educated, happy person I must follow directions and learn. She hugged me, and all was well. I went home wiser, but with my childlike vision intact.

Miss Bell, my third grade teacher, made a simple pronouncement that changed what I believed about myself. After reading my poem about purple mountains she didn't tell me it was good, or that I had done well. She said, "You are a poet!" and I believed her. With her gift of confidence, I did not doubt what I could do, or what I would do. All my poetry and creative writing that followed stemmed from the belief she inspired.

Not all my teachers sent me down my path by encouragement. When I asked Mrs. Gibb, my 8th grade Drama teacher, if I should take a drama class in high school she smiled thinly and said, "Maybe you should pursue something else, dear." I was very disappointed, but took her advice and didn't sign up for theatre. At the beginning of my 9th grade year I thought, "What does she know? She thought the Bee Gees were of the devil!" (She had serious issues sharing a last name with the Brothers Gibb!) So despite her less than stellar assessment, I auditioned for the part of "Scout" in *To Kill A Mockingbird*. Not only did I get the part, I won Best Actress for the school year. That, and I spoke with a southern accent for months after the play ended!

The rest of my high school theater

career was shaped and directed by Robyn Bishop, the teacher I fondly called "Imperious Leader." She was talented, funny, tough, and could yell like no one else. She taught me that by acting we do not act, we become. I learned to empathize with those I portrayed, to believe, to take down the walls of fear and open myself up to truth and emotion. She was the reason I wanted to become a drama teacher myself. With the help of my "Imperious Leader," I earned Best Actress twice at the regional level, once at the State level, and received two theatre scholarships.

By the time I was a college student I felt very self sufficient and independent. Broadening my studies from Theatre to include a more general Liberal Art emphasis, I thrived on subjects like Greek and Roman Mythology, Shakespeare, and Humanities. In the middle of my second semester, Mrs. Snow, my Humanities professor, asked me to tutor a student who was failing her class. I discovered I enjoyed tutoring even more than my own studying, and when my student pulled her grade up to a C+, after getting A's on the last two finals, I realized that I had become what I had admired most growing up: A teacher.

The four years I spent teaching at a private school as a Humanities/Theatre Teacher were some of the most rewarding of my professional and personal life. My students became my children, their successes and triumphs my own, and every round of applause louder because I had had a hand in it from the start.

237

The paths we walk in life do take interesting and unexpected turns. Of a necessity, my career has changed, and for now teaching is what I do on a volunteer basis, as often as I can. Yet the teachers of my past, those who served as sentinels of instruction and self realization, all taught one simple profound lesson: teaching is not a profession. Teaching is a calling. I am now part of that long line of teachers that set me on my way. Teaching is not just what we do; it is who we are—who I am. A teacher

For me to identify the most influential person and my life in terms of values and beliefs, would be no contest. My father would win hands down. But if I were to consider segments or phases of my life in which I gained specific knowledge and skills, there would be several people to credit with having a positive impact on me. I would categorize these phases of my life in the following order; childhood, college years and military service, corporate life and marriage and family.

During childhood, as with most people, my parents were a huge influence. Again, my father was the driving force behind my values and beliefs that I carry with me to some degree today. Charles Danhauer was the hardest working man I knew. He was also a World War II veteran, a member of America's greatest generation. He owned and operated his own business in the 1950s through the 1980s and employed my Mom and all six of us kids. In retrospect, many of the things that he focused on then are what large corporations of today believe to be cutting edge. His philosophy was simple, "Know your people, know your craft and know your customer, the rest takes care of itself." I believe this equates to corporations' contemporary focus on "continuously improving" people, quality, efficiency and service. Not only did my father influence me with his work ethic and business savvy, but he shared my mother's commitment to family which also impacted me a great deal. Dad earned a degree in aeronautical engineering and could have enjoyed a lucrative career while the jet age was replacing conventional aeronautics. He opted for a great marriage over a great

239

salary and began his own business rooted in his hometown of Owensboro, Kentucky. He sent all of the kids to Catholic school expecting the best spiritual and academic education. He offered college tuition for those of us who wanted to pursue our own degrees. He taught us how to respect and enjoy the beauty of the outdoors and we still carry that respect with us today. His greatest priority in life was to love his family and he showed that love by sacrificing his own wants and needs to help us be successful.

My college years and military service was a phase of my life where love was replaced with authority. I received my undergraduate degree from the University of Kentucky and my graduate degree from the University of Southern California while I was serving in the Army. There were a host of influential professors and military commanders who impacted me during this timeframe.

What was more difficult, Soviet Politics in College or Ranger School in the Army? They were both difficult, but my success or lack of success in college was a function of maturity. Authoritarian leadership was what I needed during this phase of my life and I got it. I would categorize all of my commanders together as the turning point in my maturity level as I progressed through the ranks.

The Army also exposed me to the world. I was stationed in Germany for three years and spent time in Korea and all over the United States. The experience of different cultures opened my mind to diversity of thought. I befriended many German nationals, but one in particular continues to influence me today. Manfred Auer went beyond the call of duty to ensure that I felt welcome in his country. He has a much more compassionate view of the world than most, and I credit him with altering my own views on the world. We still keep in touch and see one another on occasion. He has recently become a father and is very happy as a family man.

The beginning of corporate life also served as a wake-up call for me. As with my Army commanders, I can't single out one manager as the most influential. I would categorize all of my managers who I reported to over the years as having a major influence. They taught me that it was ok to adapt my leadership style to different corporate cultures. I've learned to take measures risks and not be ashamed of my mistakes as long as I don't repeat those mistakes. I've learned that people are your greatest asset and their success is your success . . . sounds reminiscent of my Dad's philosophy.

Marriage and family has been the most significant phase of all. My wife, Debbie, has made me truly want to be the best person that I can be. She is a very strong person and she has a strong commitment to our family. She has had a major impact on making me want to improve myself. My whole outlook on life has been elevated along with my self-confidence, my health and my job performance. I don't know where I would be or what I would be doing today without her love and support. I don't want to grow old, but I do want to grow old with her.

My son Chris is everything in a boy that I wanted to be. We call him an "old soul" because he is mature beyond his years. I enjoy seeing his grades in school which are superior to what mine were, and I love watching him excel in sports. I only attempted to be an athlete as a kid, he is one.

My daughter Sidney is as feminine a girl as a girl can be. She's strikingly pretty like her mother and I dread the coming of her teen years. If there is one person in the world I don't mind spoiling, it is Sidney. As she grows up, she is even more of a joy to be around.

Max is the youngest son just as I was. I'm amazed at how much of myself I see in him and even more amazed at how different we are. He is blessed with a very strong will that he will hopefully use to his advantage someday. Even when we are apart, the thought of his antics keeps me laughing.

Life comes full circle. It began with my father's influence during my childhood and continuous with my marriage and family. Now I know why my Dad held his values and beliefs. He must have experienced similar if not identical influences during the phases of his life that I did. I just hope that I can live up to his standard of giving. I owe that to my wife and kids.

"Why do you believe that?"

My literary agent was standing with me in the garden in the spring evening, looking past the white cherry blossoms towards the sea.

I started to answer, thinking it would be easy. She had challenged me to write something purely for myself, putting into it all the passion I had so far held in check. Now she was asking me to explain.

But it was not so simple. Not only did she not deserve a slick, unthought-of answer, I knew she would not accept one. She was inviting me to delve into myself and take apart the pieces of my belief and examine them, not unkindly, but with the utmost honesty. Would every fragment stand the test, and fit back again into a whole as beautiful as that with which I began?

She is one of the most remarkable people I have known, and she gave me a gift which enriches me still. She made me question myself without doubting myself. And there is all the difference between the two.

Under her probing I made great discoveries, cut away dead reasoning, untested assumptions, and found cleaner answers that satisfied without having to skirt around the fudged bits or fear the shadows.

Perhaps the best thing she gave me is the knowledge that that inward journey is towards the light, not the darkness. If your beliefs are worth living for, then study them all you can. The truth can take any amount of investigation. It will be stronger and more beautiful each time.

243

Questioning is not wrong, it is not faithless. The great blasphemy is not to care. To be given this marvelous, terrible and sublime world, and be indifferent to it is to deny life.

We will each find things of almost unbearable beauty along the way, emblems of our faith in the good.

There are thoughts and images that have such power for me that they have woven themselves into the fabric of my being. They stand like monoliths above the turmoil, the sun on their faces, sentinels guarding the hard won certainties of life. Their loveliness is untarnishable, intimate as my own skin, and yet as universal as humanity.

For my eyes it is always light upon water; the fire of a dying day bleeding crimson into the clouds, or the silver radiance of the moon on a misted landscape, sunrise on hoarfrost. It is the dimpled light upon sunken stones, the curl of a great wave breaking, white spume against the sky. Above all it is an empty sea with the first wing of dawn across the arch of heaven.

For my mind I am back to truth again, even when it is hard. There is cleanness to it, an honor which heals doubt and cuts away the threads of confusion. It is the courage which endures all things. It is as complete as mathematics; it defies prejudice, deceit or unreason. It is the symmetry of the atom, the splendor of a galaxy, the supreme design.

For my heart it is poetry, the chain of words which links men from all lands and ages in the sharing of our hunger and our dreams. It is passion made music as we stretch out hands through the darkness that separates us and for an instant touch one another.

For my spirit it is forgiving, when the one who, though injured, can cast away anger and find the magnitude of heart to seek the healing of the one who has inflicted the wound. It makes whole both the giver and the given, a grace which is the supreme achievement of the soul.

By these beacons I shall set my compass again and again. As long as I have them I shall not be lost for more than a space, nor forget my purpose, because I have seen where I wish to be.

Janet Haggard
Phonetic Reading Teacher

You meet the grandest people in the most unlikely places. I met Benarci Basho, his wife and grandchildren at a school bus stop, which was on a cement island surrounded with heavy college traffic. My family and I had just moved to Suisun, California. "Suisun" is a Native American word for wind and this city was appropriately named.

As my children and I approached this new bus stop for the first time, I realized how chaotic and dangerous the place was for an elementary school bus stop. It was difficult for an adult to judge timing and arrive safely on the other side.

After much frustration I managed to get my own children and the neighborhood children to the island. There I saw a well-dressed Indian grandfather or "Tata garu" with cane in hand, and his lovely wife dressed in her native clothing of India.

When I shouted a greeting over the traffic noise, the man quickly turned toward me. I was shocked to observe that he was blind. His greeting was eloquent. He introduced his wife and two grandchildren, Rahul and Shavita. He had mastered the English language and spoke beautifully in his deep, powerful voice. His wife stood quietly holding his hand.

After the bus picked up the children, I assisted this older, dignified couple back across the street. We hardly visited due to the wind and the anger I felt about that poorly placed bus stop. Within the week, after demanding that a school representative come look at this stop, the new bus stop was safely tucked into our quiet neighborhood.

Every morning, all year long, it was my

pleasure to visit with Benarci. His wife spoke no English, just beautiful Hindi, but she listened and understood some of our discussions because many times she chuckled and responded.

Benarci had been an Indian Ambassador to the United States. He was very knowledgeable, very wise. Ten years earlier, he had lost his sight when he had gone back to India on vacation and for a routine yearly eye examination. During that exam, the wrong chemicals were placed into his eyes and both corneas had ruptured causing permanent, complete blindness.

When I first heard him tell me this, I began to offer my condolences, but he immediately stopped me. "No! No!" He said. "Life really began for me when I lost my sight!" I was speechless. He went on to explain, "I had experienced much money, much power, much authority and had been so successful in the ways of the world that I spent very little time with my family. I had no lasting friendships. I prioritized all of the superficial societal events, which were mostly empty words and promises. I had too much, too many possessions and was only working too long and too hard for more."

He added, "I had never actually listened to people and what their words meant. Now, I have been forced to do so, which is a blessing in my life. I judged people on their appearances and not their hearts. Appearances mean nothing anymore. I have developed a new sense, a spiritual sense. I get to know people on a new level, a feeling level. I can feel sincerity, loyalty, honesty and their opposites.

There is much more depth and meaning in my life now. God has mercifully allowed me to finally learn how to love."

I felt that love all year long. I would try to get to the bus stop a little early just to visit and glean from the knowledge and adventures of this fine, gentle man and his devoted wife. We were all happy to see each other every morning. We laughed and cried together. We shared our different religious views and gleaned from the truths of each without contention, without argument. We became trusted friends. I learned from his newfound values. He even listened to me, a young wife and mother, wanting to learn from my experiences as well. He had truly been transformed into greatness because of his blindness.

I deem it a true honor to have known such a great soul. I wonder how I would have felt if I had only known him before his blindness? I learned from Benarci that trials can become the fuel for the heat of the furnace that can forge greatness in the hearts of the willing.

As a freshman in high school, I was duly impressed by the self-assured behavior of a transfer student who joined my class partway through the year. Pretty, bright, and articulate, Renate seemed to know almost everything. What she didn't know, she made up for in opinions. I would have given anything to be so at ease with myself. Not coming to it on my own, I thought the next best thing was to follow her example.

When Renate decided on an involved, flowery script in calligraphy class, I did the same. Here also the differences between us soon became evident. She accomplished her work with great ease while I labored at the task, feeling more and more a failure no matter how much I applied myself.

That part of the school day was sheer torture for me, because every so often, the teacher would walk up and down between the rows and check on our progress. We students idolized her. She was young and full of enthusiasm and her classes were always interesting. She taught us about the history and the evolution of writing, and which pens, paper and ink were best for different projects. Though she was a strict taskmaster, we knew that she cared. Until she married and started to raise a family, she would take five or six of us at a time to the theater, or invite us to her home for tea and cookies and discussions about anything and everything. Once in a while her mother would join us and share the viewpoint and insight of yet another generation.

To disappoint my teacher was unthinkable, yet no matter how hard I tried the results of my penmanship remained murky. I managed to escape her critical eye

249

for a time, until the day when a sinking feeling in the pit of my stomach told me that she would stop at my desk. Bending low over my work to conceal the paper did not deter her. She gently moved my arm and studied my uneven creation.

"You may have better results with something more suited to you," she suggested. "Don't let fear eclipse possibilities. Have the courage to be yourself."

That I immediately turned to another style of script and at the end of the term received an A+ from a teacher not known to give such marks is an insignificant part of the experience. Much more important were her words of encouragement. They had a lasting effect and freed me from self-imposed limitations as few other things could have done. Confidence never materializes fully formed, but little by little, I learned to trust my own instincts, my own judgment.

We all need someone to believe in our potential, because in most of us failure has a longer memory than success. It is one of the reasons why validation is especially powerful when it is given by someone we respect. To touch life at all points requires courage. Occasionally, courage comes from belonging to a group; more often, it is learned from someone we admire. Whatever the source, as my teacher used to say, "Thoughts drenched in defeat provide no foothold for your journey."

Thanks to a wise sentinel I have tried not to limit my terrain.

Index of Contributors

255